THE DEFINITIVE GUIDE TO MAKE MONEY AS A PRIVATE LENDER

A Step-by-Step Guide to Earning Active and Passive Income through Alternative Financing

EUGENE NILUS

Disclaimer

The information contained in this book, "The Definitive Guide to Making Money as a Private Lender," is for general informational purposes only. The author and publisher have made every effort to ensure the accuracy of the information as of the date of publication. However, this information is not intended to be a substitute for professional financial, legal, or tax advice.

Readers should consult with a qualified financial advisor, legal professional, or tax consultant before engaging in private lending activities or making any investment decisions. The author and publisher are not responsible for any errors or omissions, or for any outcomes related to the use of this information.

The strategies, examples, and case studies provided in this book are for illustrative purposes only. Actual results may vary based on individual circumstances, market conditions, and other factors beyond the control of the author and publisher. Private lending involves risks, including the risk of loss, and may not be suitable for all investors.

By reading this book, you agree that the author and publisher shall not be liable for any direct, indirect, incidental, or consequential damages resulting from the use of the information contained herein. The reader assumes full responsibility for their decisions and actions related to private lending.

Contact Information
For inquiries, please contact:
Eugene Nilus
eugene@y2lending.com
https://y2lending.com

This disclaimer is intended to protect the author and publisher by clarifying the scope and limitations of the information provided in the book. Readers are encouraged to seek professional advice tailored to their specific circumstances.

TABLE OF CONTENTS

CHAPTER 1

INTRODUCTION
TO PRIVATE LENDING

1.1 What is Private Lending?

Private lending is a financial arrangement where an individual or a group lends their own money to another person or business, bypassing traditional financial institutions like banks. This type of lending can offer both the lender and the borrower more flexibility and personalized terms. Let's break down this concept in a way that's easy to understand.

The Basics of Private Lending

In private lending, there are two main players:

- **Lender**: The person who lends the money.
- **Borrower**: The person who receives the money and promises to pay it back, usually with some extra money called interest.

How Does Private Lending Work?

1. **The Loan Amount**: This is the amount of money the lender gives to the borrower. It's also known as the principal.

2. **Interest Rate**: This is the extra money the borrower agrees to pay back in addition to the principal. It's often a percentage of the loan amount.

3. **Repayment Schedule**: This is the timeline over which the borrower must pay back the loan, including the interest. It can be a lump sum or in installments.

Note:

Imagine you have $100 and your friend needs to borrow it to buy a new skateboard. You agree that they will pay you back $110 in two months. That extra $10 is your interest, which compensates you for lending your money.

Why Do People Use Private Lending?

- **For Borrowers:**
  - They might not qualify for a traditional bank loan due to poor credit or lack of collateral.
  - They might need money quickly and private loans can be faster to arrange.

- **For Lenders:**
  - They can earn higher returns compared to savings accounts or other investments.
  - They have more control over who they lend to and under what terms.

Different Types of Private Loans

Private lending isn't just about lending to friends or family. Here are some common types of private loans:

1. **Personal Loans:** These are loans given to individuals for personal use, such as medical expenses, home repairs, or buying a car.

2. **Real Estate Loans:** These loans are used for buying or renovating property. The property itself usually serves as collateral.

3. **Business Loans:** These are loans given to start or expand a business. They can be secured by business assets or personal guarantees.

Understanding Interest and Profit

Interest is what makes private lending profitable for the lender. It's the extra money the borrower pays for the privilege of using the lender's money. The interest rate can vary based on several factors, including the risk of the loan and the agreed terms.

Note:

If you lend $1,000 at an interest rate of 5% per year, the borrower will pay you back $1,050 at the end of the year. Your profit is $50.

Risk in Private Lending

Every loan carries some risk, meaning there is a chance the borrower might not be able to pay back the money. This is called default. Lenders need to assess this risk carefully before agreeing to lend money. Here are some ways to manage risk:

- **Credit Check:** Checking the borrower's credit history to see how well they've repaid loans in the past.

- **Collateral:** Requiring the borrower to pledge an asset, like a car or house, which the lender can take if the loan isn't repaid.

- **Loan Terms:** Setting clear terms and conditions that protect the lender, such as higher interest rates for riskier loans.

The Role of a Lending Agreement

A lending agreement is a contract between the lender and the borrower. It outlines the terms of the loan, including the following

- Amount
- Interest rate
- Repayment schedule, and
- What happens if the borrower doesn't pay back

Having a written agreement helps prevent misunderstandings and provides legal protection.

Note:

If you lend $500 to a friend, you might write an agreement stating that they will pay you back $550 in six months. Both of you sign it to show that you agree to the terms.

Advantages of Private Lending

- **Flexibility**: You can negotiate terms that suit both you and the borrower.
- **Higher Returns:** You can earn more interest compared to traditional savings options.
- **Helping Others:** You can provide financial assistance to those who might not get it otherwise.

Disadvantages of Private Lending

- **Risk of Default:** There is always a chance the borrower may not repay the loan.

- **Time-Consuming:** Evaluating borrowers and managing loans can take a lot of time and effort.

- **Legal Complexities:** You need to be aware of the legal requirements and potential complications.

You, as a private lender, can see now how this method can be a powerful tool for making money and helping others. It requires careful consideration and management, but it can be a rewarding way to use your financial resources.

1.2 Why Become a Private Lender?

Becoming a private lender can be an attractive and profitable venture for many reasons. Let's explore various benefits and motivations for individuals to become private lenders.

1. Higher Returns

One of the main reasons people become private lenders is the potential for higher returns compared to traditional investment options like savings accounts or certificates of deposit (CDs).

- **Savings Accounts:** Banks typically offer very low interest rates on savings accounts, often less than 1%.

- **Private Loans:** As a private lender, you can charge higher interest rates, often between 5% and 15%, depending on the borrower's risk and the loan terms.

Note:

If you put $1,000 in a savings account with a 1% interest rate, you would earn $10 in a year. But if you lend the same $1,000 at a 10% interest rate, you would earn $100 in a year.

2. Flexibility and Control

Private lending allows you to have more control over your investments and lending decisions.

- **Loan Terms**: You can set the terms of the loan, including the interest rate, repayment schedule, and collateral requirements.

- **Borrower Selection**: You can choose who to lend to based on your own criteria and risk assessment.

Note:

If you want to help a local business owner who needs $5,000 to expand their store, you can agree on a loan term that suits both of you, such as a 10% interest rate with monthly payments over two years.

3. Helping Others

Private lending can be a way to support individuals or businesses in your community who may not have access to traditional bank loans.

- **Personal Loans:** You can help friends or family members who need money for personal reasons, such as medical expenses, education, or home repairs.

- **Business Loans:** You can assist small business owners or entrepreneurs who need funding to start or grow their businesses.

Note:

Your neighbor wants to start a small bakery but can't get a loan from the bank. You lend them $3,000 to buy equipment and ingredients, and they agree to pay you back with interest once the business is up and running.

4. Diversifying Your Investment Portfolio

Adding private loans to your investment portfolio can diversify your sources of income and reduce overall risk.

- **Different Asset Class**: Private loans are a different asset class compared to stocks, bonds, or real estate, providing an additional stream of income.

- **Risk Management**: By lending to multiple borrowers across different sectors, you can spread the risk and potentially reduce the impact of any single default.

Note:

You already have investments in the stock market and real estate. By lending money to a local business and a friend, you add two more income streams, which can make your overall financial situation more stable.

5. Personal Satisfaction

Private lending can provide a sense of personal satisfaction from seeing the positive impact of your loans.

- **Community Development**: You can contribute to the growth and development of your local community.

- **Success Stories**: Watching your borrowers succeed and knowing you played a part in their success can be very rewarding.

Note:

You lend money to a young entrepreneur who dreams of opening a coffee shop. A year later, the coffee shop is thriving, and the entrepreneur is grateful for your support. Seeing their success can give you a sense of pride and accomplishment.

6. Tax Benefits

In some cases, the interest income from private lending may have tax advantages compared to other types of income.

- **Interest Income**: Depending on your country's tax laws, the interest earned from private loans may be taxed at a lower rate than other types of income.

- **Deductions**: You may also be able to deduct losses from bad loans or certain expenses related to managing your lending activities.

Note:

You lend $5,000 to a borrower at a 10% interest rate, earning $500 in interest. Depending on your tax situation, this interest income might be taxed at a favorable rate, increasing your overall profit.

7. Learning and Growth Opportunities

Becoming a private lender can also be an educational experience, helping you develop financial skills and knowledge.

- **Financial Literacy**: You'll learn about assessing creditworthiness, managing risk, and understanding loan contracts.

- **Market Insight**: Engaging with different borrowers can provide insights into various industries and markets.

Note:

You start lending money to small business owners and gradually learn about different types of businesses, market trends, and financial management. This knowledge can help you make better lending decisions in the future.

Being a private lender is not just about making money, it's also about having control over your investments, helping others, and contributing to your community.

1.3 History of Private Lending

Private lending has a long and rich history that dates back thousands of years, evolving significantly over time.

Origins of Private Lending

Private lending originated in ancient civilizations where trade and agriculture were essential parts of daily life. People needed resources to plant crops, buy goods, and expand their businesses. Here's how private lending began:

- **Ancient Mesopotamia**: One of the earliest recorded instances of lending dates back to ancient Mesopotamia (around 2000 BCE). Farmers would borrow seeds from wealthy landowners and repay them with a portion of the harvest. These early loans were crucial for agricultural communities to thrive.

- **Ancient Egypt**: In ancient Egypt, grain banks existed where individuals could deposit and borrow grain. Temples often acted as lenders, providing loans to farmers and merchants. Repayments were typically made with interest in the form of additional grain.

- **Ancient Greece and Rome**: Both Greeks and Romans practiced private lending. Wealthy citizens and merchants lent money to others, often with high-interest rates. In Rome, legal contracts for loans were established, and lending became more organized.

First Recorded Private Lender

It's challenging to pinpoint the very first private lender in history, as lending practices were common in many early civilizations. However, one of the earliest recorded private lenders is Puduhepa, a powerful queen of the Hittites (around 1250 BCE). She lent large sums of silver to other rulers and merchants, showcasing an early example of influential private lending.

Evolution of Private Lending

As civilizations grew and economies became more complex, private lending evolved in several significant ways:

- **Medieval Times**: During the medieval period, private lending was often conducted by merchants and wealthy individuals. The Catholic Church initially prohibited usury (charging interest), but over time, lending with interest became more accepted, particularly among non-Christian communities like Jews and Lombards.

- **Renaissance**: The Renaissance saw the rise of banking families like the Medici in Italy. These families started as private lenders and eventually established the first banks, offering loans to traders, kings, and even the Pope. This period marked the transition from informal private lending to more formalized banking systems.

- **17th and 18th Centuries**: In Europe, the Industrial Revolution spurred a need for more capital. Private lenders played a crucial role in financing new businesses and technologies. This era saw the rise of prominent private lenders and financiers who funded everything from factories to railroads.

- **19th Century**: The 19th century was a golden age for private lending, particularly in the United States. Figures like J.P. Morgan began their careers as private lenders, providing loans to businesses and governments. Morgan's lending activities helped shape the modern financial industry.

- **20th Century**: As banks became more established, private lending continued to thrive, particularly in niche markets and among individuals and businesses that traditional banks deemed too risky. The development of legal frameworks and financial regulations provided more security and structure to private lending practices.

- **21st Century**: Today, private lending has become more accessible and diversified. With the advent of the internet, peer-to-peer lending platforms like LendingClub and Prosper have revolutionized the industry, allowing individuals to lend money directly to others without needing a traditional bank. These platforms use technology to match lenders with borrowers, streamline the lending process, and mitigate risks.

Key Historical Figures in Private Lending That You May Know

- **Puduhepa**: An early example of a private lender, lending silver in ancient times.

- **Medici Family**: A powerful banking family in Renaissance Italy, starting as private lenders and eventually establishing one of the most influential banks in Europe.

- **J.P. Morgan**: An American financier who began as a private lender and played a pivotal role in the development of the modern banking system.

Impact of Private Lending on Society

Private lending has had a profound impact on economic development throughout history:

- **Agricultural Development**: Early private loans helped farmers acquire seeds and tools, leading to better harvests and food security.

- **Commercial Expansion**: Merchants and traders used private loans to expand their businesses, facilitating trade and commerce.

- **Industrial Growth**: During the Industrial Revolution, private lenders financed new technologies and factories, driving industrialization and economic growth.

- **Innovation and Entrepreneurship**: In modern times, private lending has enabled entrepreneurs to start new businesses and innovate, contributing to job creation and economic diversity.

Private lending has always been adapting to meet the changing needs of society starting from ancient grain loans to modern peer-to-peer platforms and has had a huge influence in economic development and personal finance.

If you understand the private lending origins and evolution, it will help you appreciate the vital role it plays in today's financial landscape.

CHAPTER 2

HOW PRIVATE LENDING WORKS

2.1 The Basics of a Loan

Understanding the basics of a loan is essential for both lenders and borrowers. A loan is an agreement where one party (the lender) gives money to another party (the borrower) with the expectation that the money will be repaid, usually with interest. Below, I will break down the key components of a loan and how they work.

1. Principal

The principal is the amount of money that is being borrowed. It is the initial sum that the lender gives to the borrower.

Note:

If you lend your friend $100 to buy a new video game, the $100 is the principal.

2. Interest Rate

The interest rate is the percentage of the principal that the borrower agrees to pay in addition to repaying the principal. This is the cost of borrowing the money and is how lenders make a profit.

- **Fixed Interest Rate**: The interest rate stays the same throughout the life of the loan.

- **Variable Interest Rate**: The interest rate can change over time, usually based on market conditions.

Note:

If you lend $100 at an interest rate of 5%, your friend will pay you back $105. The extra $5 is the interest.

3. Repayment Schedule

The repayment schedule outlines how and when the borrower will repay the loan. It can vary based on the agreement between the lender and the borrower.

- **Lump Sum**: The borrower pays back the entire principal and interest at once at the end of the loan term.

- **Installments**: The borrower makes regular payments (monthly, quarterly, etc.) until the loan is fully repaid.

Note:

If your friend agrees to pay you back in two months, they might pay $52.50 each month for two months to repay the $100 principal plus $5 interest.

4. Term of the Loan

The term of the loan is the period over which the loan is to be repaid. This can range from a few weeks to several years, depending on the agreement.

Note:

A short-term loan might be for three months, while a long-term loan could be for five years.

5. Collateral

Collateral is an asset that the borrower pledges to the lender as security for the loan. If the borrower fails to repay the loan, the lender can take the collateral.

- **Secured Loan**: A loan that is backed by collateral.
- **Unsecured Loan**: A loan that does not require collateral.

Note:

If you lend $1,000 to your friend to buy a car and the car itself is the collateral, you can take the car if they don't repay the loan.

6. Loan Agreement

A loan agreement is a document that outlines the terms and conditions of the loan. It is important to have a written agreement to prevent misunderstandings and provide legal protection for both parties.

Key elements of a loan agreement include:

- The principal amount
- The interest rate
- The repayment schedule
- The term of the loan
- Any collateral required
- Penalties for late payments or default

Note:

You and your friend write down the terms of the $100 loan, including the 5% interest and the two-month repayment period, and both of you sign it.

7. Default and Penalties

Default occurs when the borrower fails to repay the loan according to the agreed terms. Penalties are consequences outlined in the loan agreement for late payments or failure to repay.

Note:

If your friend doesn't pay back the $100 loan on time, the agreement might include a penalty fee of an extra $10.

Understanding the Loan Process

The loan process typically involves several steps:

1. **Application**: The borrower applies for a loan by providing information about their financial situation and the purpose of the loan.

2. **Evaluation**: The lender evaluates the borrower's creditworthiness, which may include checking credit scores and assessing collateral.

3. **Approval**: If the lender decides the borrower is a good risk, the loan is approved, and the terms are agreed upon.

4. **Disbursement**: The lender gives the principal amount to the borrower.

5. **Repayment**: The borrower makes payments according to the repayment schedule until the loan is fully repaid.

Note:

You can now see how each component plays a critical role in the lending process. Whether you are lending or borrowing, knowing these basics helps ensure that loans are managed effectively and that both parties benefit from the arrangement.

2.2 Types of Private Loans

Private loans can be tailored to meet a variety of needs, offering flexibility and opportunities for both lenders and borrowers. This subchapter explores different types of private loans, explaining their purposes, benefits, and typical terms.

1. Personal Loans

Personal loans are used for individual needs and can cover a wide range of expenses.

- **Purpose**: Personal loans can be used for medical bills, home repairs, vacations, weddings, or any other personal expenses.

- **Terms**: These loans usually have fixed interest rates and repayment periods, typically ranging from a few months to several years.

Note:

2. Real Estate Loans

Real estate loans are used to purchase or renovate properties. These loans are often substantial and come with specific terms related to the property.

- **Purpose**: Buying a home, purchasing investment properties, or renovating existing real estate.

- **Terms**: These loans often have longer terms, ranging from 15 to 30 years, with either fixed or adjustable interest rates. The property usually serves as collateral.

Note:

You want to buy a small rental property for $200,000. A private lender offers you a real estate loan with a 20-year term and a fixed interest rate. The property itself is used as collateral.

3. Business Loans

Business loans are designed to help entrepreneurs start, grow, or manage their businesses.

- **Purpose**: Financing startup costs, expanding operations, purchasing equipment, or managing cash flow.

- **Terms**: Business loans can vary widely in amount and term, depending on the business's needs and the lender's criteria. They may be secured by business assets or personal guarantees.

Note:

You want to open a bakery and need $50,000 for equipment and initial operating costs. A private lender provides you with a business loan to be repaid over five years, using your business assets as collateral.

4. Bridge Loans

Bridge loans are short-term loans that provide temporary financing until permanent financing can be secured or an existing obligation is removed.

- **Purpose**: Often used in real estate transactions to bridge the gap between buying a new property and selling an existing one.

- **Terms**: These loans are usually for short periods, from a few months to a year, and often have higher interest rates due to their short-term nature.

Note:

You find a perfect new house but haven't sold your current home yet. A private lender offers you a bridge loan to buy the new house. Once you sell your old home, you repay the bridge loan.

5. Peer-to-Peer (P2P) Loans

P2P loans are facilitated through online platforms that match borrowers with individual lenders.

- **Purpose**: These loans can be for personal, business, or other purposes and are typically unsecured.

- **Terms**: The terms vary based on the platform, borrower's creditworthiness, and the amount borrowed. Interest rates and repayment periods are determined by the platform's algorithms and investor preferences.

Note:

You need $10,000 to consolidate credit card debt. You apply on a P2P lending platform, and several individual investors collectively fund your loan, which you repay over three years at a fixed interest rate.

6. Microloans

Microloans are small loans, often provided to entrepreneurs or small businesses, particularly in developing countries.

- **Purpose**: Helping small business owners or entrepreneurs who lack access to traditional banking services.
- **Terms**: These loans are usually small (often less than $50,000) and have short repayment periods. Interest rates can vary.

Note:

A small farmer needs $1,000 to buy seeds and tools for the planting season. A private lender offers a microloan to be repaid after the harvest.

7. Hard Money Loans

Hard money loans are a type of real estate loan typically used for investment properties. These loans are secured by the property and are often used by real estate investors for quick financing.

- **Purpose**: Purchasing, flipping, or refinancing investment properties.
- **Terms**: These loans usually have higher interest rates and shorter terms (typically 1-3 years) compared to traditional

mortgages. They are often based more on the value of the property than the borrower's creditworthiness.

Note:

A real estate investor needs $150,000 to purchase and renovate a fixer-upper. A hard money lender offers a loan secured by the property with a one-year term and a high interest rate.

8. Family and Friends Loans

Loans from family and friends are informal loans where the lender is someone the borrower knows personally.

- **Purpose**: These loans can be for any purpose, including personal expenses, starting a business, or buying a home.

- **Terms**: Terms are flexible and based on the personal relationship. It's important to have a clear agreement to avoid misunderstandings.

Note:

You borrow $3,000 from your uncle to help pay for college tuition. You both agree that you will repay him over the next two years without interest.

9. Invoice Financing

Invoice financing involves selling unpaid invoices to a lender in exchange for immediate cash. This type of loan helps businesses manage cash flow issues.

- **Purpose**: Providing working capital based on outstanding invoices.

- **Terms**: The lender advances a percentage of the invoice amount (usually 70-90%) and collects the payment from the customer. The remaining amount, minus fees, is returned to the business once the invoice is paid.

Note:

Your business has $10,000 in unpaid invoices. A private lender offers invoice financing, giving you $8,000 upfront and collecting the invoices directly from your customers.

By understanding the different types of private loans, both lenders and borrowers can make informed decisions that best suit their financial needs and goals. Each type of loan has its own set of benefits and considerations, making it essential to choose the right one for your specific situation.

2.3 Understanding Risk

Risk is an inherent part of lending, and understanding it is crucial for private lenders. Let's explore the different types of risks associated with private lending, how to assess and manage them, and strategies to mitigate potential losses.

1. Types of Risk

There are several types of risks that private lenders need to be aware of:

- **Credit Risk**: The risk that the borrower will not repay the loan as agreed. This is the most common risk in lending.

- **Collateral Risk**: The risk that the value of the collateral will decrease, making it insufficient to cover the loan if the borrower defaults.

- **Interest Rate Risk**: The risk that changes in interest rates will affect the profitability of the loan.

- **Liquidity Risk**: The risk that the lender will not be able to easily convert the loan into cash without a significant loss.

- **Operational Risk**: The risk of loss due to failed internal processes, systems, or external events, such as legal issues or fraud.

2. Assessing Risk

To manage risk effectively, lenders must assess the potential risk associated with each loan. Here are some key steps in assessing risk:

- **Creditworthiness**: Evaluate the borrower's ability to repay the loan. This includes checking their credit score, income, employment history, and existing debts.

Note:

Before lending $5,000 to a friend for their business, you check their credit report to ensure they have a history of repaying debts on time.

- **Collateral Evaluation**: If the loan is secured, assess the value and quality of the collateral. Ensure that it is sufficient to cover the loan amount if the borrower defaults.

Note:

If you are lending $50,000 for a real estate investment, you might hire an appraiser to determine the current market value of the property being used as collateral.

- **Loan Terms**: Consider the terms of the loan, such as the interest rate, repayment schedule, and loan duration. Shorter loans with higher interest rates typically carry more risk but offer quicker returns.

Note:

A two-year loan with a 10% interest rate might be riskier than a five-year loan with a 5% interest rate, but it will generate returns faster.

- **Market Conditions**: Analyze the broader economic environment and industry-specific conditions that could impact the borrower's ability to repay the loan.

Note:

If lending to a construction business, consider the current state of the real estate market and economic indicators that affect construction demand.

3. Managing Risk

Once risks have been assessed, lenders can take steps to manage and mitigate them:

- **Diversification**: Spread your investments across multiple loans and borrowers to reduce the impact of any single default.

Note:

Instead of lending $100,000 to one borrower, you might lend $10,000 to ten different borrowers in various industries.

- **Loan-to-Value Ratio (LTV)**: Limit the amount you lend based on the value of the collateral. A lower LTV ratio means more protection if the borrower defaults.

Note:

If the collateral is a property worth $200,000, you might limit the loan to $150,000 to ensure a buffer in case property values drop.

- **Interest Rates and Fees**: Charge higher interest rates and fees for riskier loans to compensate for the increased risk.

Note:

If lending to a borrower with a lower credit score, you might charge a higher interest rate to offset the greater chance of default.

- **Legal Protections**: Use legally binding contracts and ensure all loan agreements are clearly documented. This provides legal recourse in case of default.

Note:

Include a clause in the loan agreement that allows you to take possession of the collateral if the borrower fails to make payments.

- **Insurance**: Purchase insurance policies that can protect against certain risks, such as property insurance for real estate loans or credit insurance for personal loans.

Note:

If you are lending for home renovation, require the borrower to have homeowner's insurance that covers the cost of the renovation.

4. Monitoring and Reviewing Loans

Ongoing monitoring and regular review of your loans are essential for effective risk management:

- **Regular Check-ins**: Maintain communication with borrowers to stay informed about their financial situation and any potential issues.

Note:

Schedule monthly / quarterly meetings or calls with borrowers to discuss their progress and any challenges they face.

- **Payment Tracking**: Keep detailed records of payments received and due dates. Promptly follow up on late payments to prevent defaults.

Note:

Use financial software to track loan payments and send automatic reminders to borrowers before payment due dates.

- **Adjusting Terms**: Be open to renegotiating loan terms if a borrower is facing temporary financial difficulties. This can help prevent defaults and maintain the relationship.

Note:

If a borrower loses their job but expects to find new employment soon, you might temporarily reduce their monthly payments until they are back on their feet.

5. Examples of Risk Management

Here are a few scenarios demonstrating how risk management strategies can be applied:

Scenario 1: Personal Loan to a Friend

- **Assessment**: Check your friend's credit score and employment status.

- **Management**: Agree on a short-term loan with a higher interest rate. Write a formal loan agreement and include a cosigner if possible.

- **Monitoring**: Schedule monthly check-ins to ensure timely payments.

Scenario 2: Real Estate Loan

- **Assessment**: Appraise the property and verify the borrower's income and credit history.

- **Management**: Set a low LTV ratio, require property insurance, get added as a loss payee to their property insurance, use a legally binding mortgage agreement, note, and a personal guarantee.

- **Monitoring**: Track property values and review the borrower's financial statements annually.

Scenario 3: Business Loan

- **Assessment**: Analyze the business's financial statements, market conditions, and the borrower's business plan.

- **Management**: Diversify your investment by lending to multiple businesses, charge a higher interest rate, and require a personal guarantee.

- **Monitoring**: Review quarterly financial reports from the business and hold periodic meetings with the business owner.

By managing the risks associated with private lending, you, as a private lender, can make informed decisions that protect your investment and increase the likelihood of successful loan repayments.

This proactive approach ensures that you can enjoy the benefits of private lending while minimizing potential downsides.

CHAPTER 3

ACTIVE VS.
PASSIVE PRIVATE LENDING

3.1 Active Private Lender

Being an active private lender involves directly managing your lending activities engaging with borrowers, and overseeing the entire loan process

Let's see what it means to be an active private lender, including the benefits and challenges, the skills required, and practical tips for success.

1. What is an Active Private Lender?

An active private lender is someone who takes a hands-on approach to their lending business. This means they are involved in every step of the lending process, from finding and evaluating potential borrowers to negotiating loan terms and managing repayments.

Responsibilities of an Active Private Lender:

- **Finding Borrowers**: Actively seeking out individuals or businesses in need of loans.

- **Evaluating Applications**: Assessing the creditworthiness and financial stability of potential borrowers.

- **Negotiating Terms**: Setting interest rates, repayment schedules, and other loan terms.

- **Managing Disbursement**: Ensuring that loan funds are distributed correctly and promptly.

- **Monitoring Repayments**: Keeping track of payments and addressing any issues that arise.

- **Handling Defaults**: Taking appropriate action if a borrower fails to repay the loan, which may include legal proceedings or seizing collateral.

2. Benefits of Being an Active Private Lender

Being actively involved in your lending business can offer several advantages:

- **Higher Returns**: Active lenders often have the opportunity to earn higher returns by carefully selecting borrowers and negotiating favorable loan terms.

- **Control Over Investments**: By managing every aspect of the lending process, you have more control over your investments and can make decisions that align with your risk tolerance and financial goals.

- **Relationship Building**: Engaging directly with borrowers allows you to build strong relationships, which can lead to repeat business and referrals.

- **Flexibility**: Active lenders can tailor loan terms and conditions to meet the specific needs of borrowers, potentially increasing the attractiveness of their loans.

Note:

Imagine you lend $50,000 to a small business owner to expand their café. By actively managing this loan, you can set a higher interest rate based on the borrower's strong credit history, ensure that the loan is secured with valuable collateral, and maintain regular communication to monitor the business's progress.

3. Challenges of Being an Active Private Lender

While there are many benefits to being an active private lender, there are also challenges to consider:

- **Time Commitment**: Managing loans actively requires a significant amount of time and effort. This can be demanding, especially if you have multiple loans to oversee.

- **Risk of Default**: Even with careful evaluation, there is always a risk that borrowers may default on their loans. Active lenders must be prepared to handle such situations.

- **Legal and Regulatory Knowledge**: Active lenders need to be familiar with the legal and regulatory aspects of lending to ensure compliance and protect their investments.

- **Stress Management**: Dealing with borrowers, especially those who are struggling to repay, can be stressful. Effective communication and problem-solving skills are essential.

4. Skills Required for Active Private Lending

To be a successful active private lender, several key skills and attributes are important:

- **Financial Acumen**: Understanding financial statements, credit reports, and market conditions to assess the risk and viability of loans.

- **Negotiation Skills**: Being able to negotiate favorable loan terms while maintaining good relationships with borrowers.

- **Attention to Detail**: Carefully reviewing loan applications, agreements, and repayment schedules to avoid mistakes and ensure accuracy.

- **Communication Skills**: Effectively communicating with borrowers, legal advisors, and other stakeholders.

- **Problem-Solving Abilities**: Quickly addressing issues that arise during the loan term, such as late payments or changes in the borrower's financial situation.

Note:

As an active private lender, you might receive a loan application from a startup seeking $100,000. Your financial acumen helps you analyze their business plan and financial projections, while your negotiation skills allow you to set an interest rate and repayment terms that balance risk and reward.

5. Practical Tips for Success

Here are some practical tips to help you succeed as an active private lender:

- **Develop a Clear Strategy**: Define your lending goals, target borrowers, and risk tolerance. Having a clear strategy will guide your lending decisions and help you stay focused.

Note:

Decide whether you want to specialize in personal loans, real estate loans, or business loans, and tailor your approach accordingly.

- **Build a Network**: Connect with other lenders, financial advisors, and industry professionals. A strong network can provide valuable insights, referrals, and support.

Note:

Join local business associations or online lending forums to meet potential borrowers and fellow lenders.

- **Stay Informed**: Keep up-to-date with market trends, economic conditions, and regulatory changes that could impact your lending business.

Note:

Subscribe to financial news sources and attend industry conferences to stay informed about the latest developments.

- **Use Technology**: Leverage financial software and online platforms to streamline your lending operations, track payments, and manage communications with borrowers.

Note:

Use a loan management software to automate payment reminders and generate financial reports.

- **Establish Clear Policies**: Create clear policies for evaluating loan applications, setting terms, and handling defaults. This will help you maintain consistency and professionalism in your lending business.

Note:

Develop a checklist for assessing creditworthiness and a standard loan agreement template to ensure all key terms are covered.

- **Monitor Loans Diligently**: Regularly review the performance of your loans and stay in contact with borrowers. Early detection of potential issues allows for proactive management.

Note:

Schedule quarterly reviews of each loan to assess repayment progress and identify any warning signs of financial distress.

By understanding the role and responsibilities of an active private lender, and by implementing these practical tips, you, as a private lender, can effectively manage your lending business, maximize returns, and build strong relationships with borrowers.

This hands-on approach requires dedication and skill but can be highly rewarding both financially and personally.

3.2 Passive Private Lender

Being a passive private lender involves delegating the majority of lending activities to third-party platforms or professionals, allowing you to invest in loans with minimal involvement.

Let's explore the concept of passive private lending, including its benefits, challenges, and strategies for success.

1. What is a Passive Private Lender?

A passive private lender is someone who invests in loans without actively participating in the lending process. Instead of directly managing loans, passive lenders rely on intermediaries such as online lending platforms, investment funds, or private lending syndicates to handle loan origination, underwriting, and servicing.

Responsibilities of a Passive Private Lender:

- **Research and Due Diligence**: Conducting research to identify reputable lending platforms or investment opportunities.

- **Investment Allocation**: Allocating capital to different loans or investment vehicles based on risk tolerance and investment objectives.

- **Monitoring Performance**: Monitoring the performance of loans or investments and making adjustments as needed.

- **Risk Management**: Understanding and managing risks associated with passive lending, such as credit risk and market risk.

2. Benefits of Being a Passive Private Lender

Passive private lending offers several benefits for investors seeking to generate passive income and diversify their investment portfolios:

- **Minimal Time Commitment**: Passive lenders can invest in loans with minimal time and effort, allowing them to focus on other priorities or pursuits.

- **Diversification**: By investing in a range of loans or investment vehicles, passive lenders can spread their risk and potentially enhance returns.

- **Access to Expertise**: Passive lenders can leverage the expertise of lending professionals or investment managers to identify and evaluate opportunities.

- **Potential for Passive Income**: Passive private lending can provide a steady stream of passive income through interest payments and investment returns.

- **Flexibility**: Passive lenders have the flexibility to choose their level of involvement and adjust their investment strategy as needed.

Note:

A passive private lender allocates a portion of their investment portfolio to a peer-to-peer lending platform, allowing them to earn passive income from interest payments without actively managing individual loans.

3. Challenges of Being a Passive Private Lender

While passive private lending offers several advantages, there are also challenges and considerations to keep in mind:

- **Limited Control**: Passive lenders have limited control over the loan origination process, underwriting criteria, and loan servicing, which can impact the quality of investments.

- **Dependency on Intermediaries**: Passive lenders rely on third-party platforms or professionals to manage lending activities, increasing the risk of fraud, mismanagement, or platform failure.

- **Market Volatility**: Passive lenders are exposed to market fluctuations and economic downturns, which can affect the performance of loans or investment vehicles.

- **Risk of Loss**: Despite diversification efforts, passive lenders still face the risk of investment losses, particularly in the event of borrower defaults or economic crises.

4. Strategies for Success as a Passive Private Lender

To mitigate risks and maximize returns as a passive private lender, consider the following strategies:

- **Diversification**: Allocate capital across a range of loans or investment vehicles to spread risk and minimize the impact of individual defaults.

Note:

Invest in loans with varying risk profiles, geographic locations, and borrower demographics to diversify your portfolio.

- **Due Diligence**: Conduct thorough due diligence on lending platforms or investment opportunities to assess their track record, reputation, and risk management practices.

Note:

Research the performance metrics, historical returns, and borrower default rates of peer-to-peer lending platforms before investing.

- **Risk Management**: Implement risk management strategies, such as setting investment limits, monitoring performance metrics, and adjusting allocations based on market conditions.

Note:

Set a maximum exposure limit for each loan or investment vehicle to prevent overexposure to any single risk factor.

- **Stay Informed**: Stay informed about industry trends, regulatory changes, and macroeconomic factors that could impact the performance of loans or investment vehicles.

Note:

Subscribe to industry publications, attend webinars or conferences, and consult with financial advisors to stay up-to-date.

- **Regular Review**: Regularly review the performance of your investments, monitor key metrics, and reassess your investment strategy as needed.

Note:

Conduct quarterly reviews of your portfolio, analyze investment returns, and make adjustments based on performance trends.

By adopting these strategies, passive private lenders can navigate the complexities of passive lending, mitigate risks, and optimize returns over time.

While passive lending requires less active involvement compared to traditional lending, it still requires careful planning, diligence, and ongoing monitoring to achieve investment objectives and financial success.

To explore opportunities as a passive private lender, check out us out at:

https://y2lending.com/invest

CHAPTER 4

SETTING UP
AS A PRIVATE LENDER

4.1 Legal Requirements

Engaging in private lending involves complying with various legal requirements to ensure that your lending activities are conducted ethically, transparently, and in accordance with applicable laws and regulations.

Let's take a look at some of the key legal considerations for private lenders, including licensing, regulatory compliance, and contractual obligations.

1. Licensing and Registration

In many jurisdictions, private lending activities are subject to licensing and registration requirements. Before engaging in private lending, it is essential to research and understand the legal requirements in your jurisdiction to ensure compliance. This may involve obtaining licenses from regulatory authorities or registering with relevant agencies.

Note:

In the United States, private lenders may need to obtain licenses from state regulatory agencies or comply with federal regulations such as the Securities Act of 1933 and the Dodd-Frank Wall Street Reform and Consumer Protection Act.

2. Regulatory Compliance

Private lenders must adhere to various laws and regulations governing lending practices, consumer protection, and financial transactions. These regulations are designed to safeguard the interests of borrowers, prevent predatory lending practices, and maintain the integrity of the financial system.

Key Regulatory Areas for Private Lenders:

- **Usury Laws**: Laws that regulate the maximum allowable interest rates on loans to prevent excessive interest charges.

- **Truth in Lending Act (TILA)**: Requires lenders to disclose key terms and costs of loans to borrowers, including annual percentage rates (APRs) and total loan costs.

- **Fair Lending Laws**: Prohibit discrimination in lending based on factors such as race, ethnicity, gender, or age.

- **Privacy Laws**: Protect the privacy and confidentiality of borrower information and financial data.

- **Anti-Money Laundering (AML) Laws**: Require lenders to implement measures to prevent money laundering and terrorist financing activities.

Note:

A private lender must ensure that loan agreements comply with TILA requirements by providing borrowers with accurate disclosures of loan terms, including interest rates, fees, and repayment schedules.

3. Contractual Obligations

Private lending transactions are typically governed by contractual agreements between lenders and borrowers. These contracts outline the rights, responsibilities, and obligations of each party, as well as the terms and conditions of the loan. It is crucial to draft clear, comprehensive loan agreements that address key legal and financial aspects of the lending arrangement.

Key Components of Loan Agreements:

- **Loan Amount and Terms**: Specify the principal amount, interest rate, repayment schedule, and any other relevant terms of the loan.

- **Collateral**: Describe the collateral securing the loan, including its value, condition, and method of valuation.

- **Default and Remedies**: Define the circumstances under which the borrower will be considered in default and outline the lender's rights and remedies in the event of default.

- **Governing Law and Jurisdiction**: Determine the applicable law governing the loan agreement and the jurisdiction for resolving disputes.

- **Disclosure Requirements**: Ensure compliance with legal disclosure requirements, including TILA disclosures and other regulatory mandates.

Note:

A private lender enters into a loan agreement with a borrower, specifying a $50,000 loan amount, a 10% interest rate, and a repayment term of two years. The agreement also includes provisions for collateralizing the loan with the borrower's property and outlines the lender's rights in case of default.

4. Legal Documentation and Recordkeeping

Maintaining accurate and comprehensive legal documentation is essential for private lenders to protect their interests, demonstrate compliance with legal requirements, and enforce contractual obligations. Lenders should keep detailed records of loan agreements, disclosures, payments, correspondence, and other relevant documentation.

Note:

A private lender maintains a complete file for each loan transaction, including copies of loan agreements, borrower information, payment records, and correspondence, to ensure compliance with legal and regulatory requirements.

5. Legal Counsel and Professional Advice

Given the complex legal landscape surrounding private lending, seeking legal counsel and professional advice is advisable for private lenders. Legal experts can help lenders navigate legal challenges, mitigate legal risks effectively, and provide guidance on:

- regulatory compliance
- contract drafting
- risk management
- dispute resolution

By complying with legal requirements, you, as a private lender, can conduct your lending activities responsibly, mitigate legal risks, and build trust and credibility with borrowers, regulatory authorities, and other stakeholders.

Prioritizing legal compliance and adherence to ethical standards is essential for long-term success and sustainability in the private lending industry.

4.2 Creating a Lending Agreement

A lending agreement is a legally binding contract that outlines the terms and conditions of a loan between a lender and a borrower. This subchapter explores the key components of a lending agreement, including loan terms, repayment schedules, collateral, default provisions, and other important considerations.

1. Loan Terms and Conditions

The loan terms and conditions section of a lending agreement defines the key parameters of the loan, including:

- **Loan Amount:** The principal amount being lent to the borrower.

- **Interest Rate:** The rate at which interest will accrue on the loan.

- **Repayment Schedule:** The timeline for repaying the loan, including the frequency and amount of payments.

- **Loan Term:** The duration of the loan, typically expressed in months or years.

- **Purpose of the Loan:** The intended use of the loan proceeds by the borrower.

Note:

A lending agreement specifies that the lender will provide a $10,000 loan to the borrower at an annual interest rate of 8%, with monthly payments of $200 over a five-year term.

2. Collateral

If the loan is secured, the lending agreement should include details about the collateral that the borrower is providing to secure the loan. This may include:

- **Description of Collateral:** A detailed description of the collateral, including its type, value, and condition.

- **Valuation Method:** The method used to determine the value of the collateral, such as an independent appraisal.

- **Security Interest:** The borrower's agreement to grant the lender a security interest in the collateral to secure repayment of the loan.

Note:

A lending agreement for a real estate loan includes a legal description of the property being used as collateral, an appraisal report confirming its value, and a provision granting the lender a mortgage or deed of trust on the property.

3. Default Provisions

The lending agreement should outline the circumstances under which the borrower will be considered in default and the remedies available to the lender in case of default. This may include:

- **Events of Default:** Specific events or conditions that constitute default, such as failure to make timely payments or breach of other loan covenants.

- **Remedies:** The lender's rights and remedies in the event of default, including acceleration of the loan, foreclosure on collateral, or pursuit of legal action.

Note:

4. Representations and Warranties

The borrower may be required to make certain representations and warranties in the lending agreement, providing assurances to the lender regarding their financial condition, legal status, and ability to repay the loan. This may include:

- **Financial Statements:** The borrower's representation that their financial statements are accurate and complete.

- **Legal Compliance:** The borrower's representation that they are in compliance with all applicable laws and regulations.

- **Title and Ownership:** The borrower's representation that they have legal title to any collateral provided and have the right to pledge it as security for the loan.

Note:

5. Governing Law and Jurisdiction

The lending agreement should specify the governing law that will govern the interpretation and enforcement of the agreement, as well as the jurisdiction where disputes will be resolved. This helps ensure clarity and predictability in the event of legal proceedings.

Note:

A lending agreement states that it will be governed by the laws of the state where the lender is located and that any disputes arising under the agreement will be resolved through arbitration in accordance with the rules of the American Arbitration Association.

6. Execution and Signatures

The lending agreement should be executed by both parties with signatures to indicate their acceptance and agreement to be bound by the terms and conditions of the agreement. Each party should retain a signed copy of the agreement for their records.

Note:

The lending agreement includes signature blocks for both the lender and the borrower, with space for the date of execution.

By creating a comprehensive lending agreement that addresses these key components, you, as a private lender, can establish clear expectations, protect your interests, and mitigate risks associated with lending activities.

It is important to consult with legal professionals to ensure that the agreement complies with applicable laws and regulations and adequately addresses the unique circumstances of the loan transaction.

CHAPTER 5

EVALUATING BORROWERS

5.1 Credit Scores and Reports

Understanding credit scores and reports is crucial for private lenders as they assess the creditworthiness of potential borrowers. This subchapter delves into the basics of credit scores and reports, how they are calculated, their significance in lending decisions, and how to interpret them effectively.

1. What are Credit Scores and Reports?

Credit Score:

A credit score is a numerical representation of a borrower's creditworthiness, typically ranging from 300 to 850. It is used by lenders to evaluate the likelihood that a borrower will repay their debts. Higher scores indicate better creditworthiness.

Credit Report:

A credit report is a detailed record of a borrower's credit history, compiled by credit bureaus. It includes information about credit accounts, payment history, outstanding debts, and public records such as bankruptcies or foreclosures.

Note:

A borrower with a credit score of 750 is considered to have good credit, while a borrower with a score of 600 may be seen as a higher risk.

2. How are Credit Scores Calculated?

Credit scores are calculated using several factors, each contributing a specific percentage to the overall score. The most commonly used scoring model is the FICO score, which is calculated as follows:

- **Payment History (35%)**: The borrower's record of on-time or late payments.

- **Amounts Owed (30%)**: The total amount of debt the borrower currently owes.

- **Length of Credit History (15%)**: The length of time the borrower has had credit accounts.

- **Credit Mix (10%)**: The variety of credit accounts, such as credit cards, mortgages, and installment loans.

- **New Credit (10%)**: Recent credit inquiries and newly opened accounts.

Note:

A borrower with a long history of on-time payments, low outstanding debt, and a diverse mix of credit accounts will likely have a high credit score.

3. The Importance of Credit Scores in Lending Decisions

Credit scores play a significant role in lending decisions for several reasons:

- **Risk Assessment**: Credit scores help lenders assess the risk of lending to a borrower. Higher scores suggest lower risk.

- **Interest Rates**: Borrowers with higher credit scores typically qualify for lower interest rates, reducing the cost of borrowing.

- **Loan Approval**: Many lenders have minimum credit score requirements for loan approval. Borrowers with scores below the threshold may be denied.

Note:

A private lender may decide to offer a lower interest rate to a borrower with a credit score of 800 compared to a borrower with a score of 650, reflecting the lower risk associated with the higher score.

4. How to Interpret Credit Reports

Interpreting credit reports involves analyzing the information provided by credit bureaus to understand a borrower's financial behavior and history. Key sections of a credit report include:

- **Personal Information**: Name, address, social security number, and employment history.

- **Credit Accounts**: Details of current and past credit accounts, including account type, credit limit, balance, and payment history.

- **Public Records**: Information on bankruptcies, foreclosures, liens, and judgments.

- **Credit Inquiries**: A record of who has requested the borrower's credit report and when.

Steps to Interpret a Credit Report:

1. **Verify Personal Information**: Ensure the report accurately reflects the borrower's personal information.

2. **Review Account Details**: Examine each credit account for the amount owed, payment history, and account status.

3. **Check for Negative Items**: Identify any negative items such as late payments, collections, or public records.

4. **Analyze Credit Inquiries**: Look at recent inquiries to see how frequently the borrower has applied for credit.

Note:

A private lender reviewing a credit report might notice a history of late payments on a borrower's credit card account. This could signal potential risk and influence the lending decision.

5. Limitations of Credit Scores and Reports

While credit scores and reports are valuable tools, they have limitations that lenders should be aware of:

- **Incomplete Information**: Credit reports may not include all financial obligations, such as certain types of loans or debts that are not reported to credit bureaus.

- **Errors and Discrepancies**: Mistakes can occur in credit reports, and borrowers may have inaccurate information that affects their credit scores.

- **Context of Credit Behavior**: Credit scores do not provide context for why a borrower may have missed payments or accumulated debt.

Note:

A borrower may have a lower credit score due to medical debt or a temporary financial hardship. Understanding the context can help lenders make more informed decisions.

6. Best Practices for Using Credit Scores and Reports

To effectively use credit scores and reports in lending decisions, consider the following best practices:

- **Comprehensive Evaluation**: Use credit scores and reports as part of a broader assessment that includes income verification, employment history, and other financial metrics.

- **Verify Information**: Cross-check information provided by borrowers with their credit reports to ensure accuracy.

- **Consider the Whole Picture**: Take into account the borrower's overall financial situation and any extenuating circumstances that may affect their credit history.

- **Stay Updated**: Regularly review and update your understanding of credit scoring models and reporting practices to make informed lending decisions.

Note:

A private lender evaluates a borrower's credit report alongside their income statements and employment history, gaining a comprehensive understanding of the borrower's financial health before approving a loan.

5.2 Assessing Risk

Assessing risk is a crucial aspect of private lending, as it helps lenders determine the likelihood of borrower default and the potential impact on their investment.

Let's explore some of the various factors that contribute to risk assessment, methodologies for evaluating risk, and strategies for mitigating risk in lending decisions.

1. Factors Influencing Risk Assessment

Several factors influence the assessment of risk in private lending, including the borrower's financial health, the nature of the loan, and external economic conditions. Key factors to consider are:

- **Creditworthiness**: The borrower's credit score and credit history provide insights into their past borrowing behavior and likelihood of repaying the loan.

- **Income and Employment Stability**: The borrower's income level, employment status, and job stability affect their ability to make consistent loan payments.

- **Debt-to-Income Ratio (DTI)**: The ratio of the borrower's total monthly debt payments to their gross monthly income. A lower DTI indicates better financial health and less risk.

- **Loan Purpose**: The intended use of the loan funds, such as for real estate investment, business expansion, or personal expenses, can impact the risk level.

- **Collateral**: The presence and value of collateral securing the loan reduce the lender's risk by providing a tangible asset that can be claimed in case of default.

- **Economic Conditions**: Broader economic factors, such as interest rates, inflation, and employment rates, can influence the risk associated with lending.

Note:

A borrower with a high credit score, stable employment, and a low DTI ratio presents a lower risk compared to a borrower with a lower credit score, unstable job history, and high DTI ratio.

2. Methodologies for Evaluating Risk

Private lenders can use various methodologies to evaluate risk, combining quantitative analysis with qualitative judgment to make informed lending decisions. Key methodologies include:

- **Credit Analysis**: Reviewing the borrower's credit report and credit score to assess their creditworthiness and identify any red flags, such as late payments or high credit utilization.

- **Financial Analysis**: Analyzing the borrower's financial statements, including income, expenses, assets, and liabilities, to understand their financial health and ability to repay the loan.

- **Cash Flow Analysis**: Evaluating the borrower's cash flow to ensure they have sufficient income to cover loan payments, especially for business loans or real estate investments.

- **Loan-to-Value Ratio (LTV)**: Calculating the LTV ratio for secured loans by dividing the loan amount by the value of the collateral. A lower LTV ratio indicates lower risk.

- **Scenario Analysis**: Assessing how different scenarios, such as changes in interest rates or economic downturns, could impact the borrower's ability to repay the loan.

Note:

A lender performs a cash flow analysis for a business loan applicant, reviewing the company's income statements and cash flow projections to ensure it can generate enough revenue to meet loan obligations.

3. Strategies for Mitigating Risk

To mitigate risk and protect their investments, private lenders can implement various risk management strategies, including:

- **Diversification**: Spreading investments across multiple borrowers, industries, and loan types to reduce the impact of any single default.

- **Collateralization**: Securing loans with valuable collateral, such as real estate or equipment, to provide a safety net in case of borrower default.

- **Loan Structuring**: Structuring loans with terms and conditions that align with the borrower's financial situation and ability to repay, such as adjustable interest rates or flexible repayment schedules.

- **Credit Enhancements**: Using credit enhancements, such as personal guarantees or co-signers, to improve the borrower's credit profile and reduce lender risk.

- **Regular Monitoring**: Continuously monitoring the borrower's financial health and loan performance, allowing the lender to take proactive measures if risk levels increase.

Note:

A private lender diversifies their portfolio by lending to borrowers in different industries, securing loans with real estate collateral, and requiring personal guarantees for higher-risk loans.

4. Tools and Resources for Risk Assessment

Private lenders can leverage various tools and resources to enhance their risk assessment capabilities and make data-driven decisions:

- **Credit Scoring Models**: Utilizing credit scoring models, such as FICO or VantageScore, to quantify borrower creditworthiness and compare risk levels.

- **Financial Software**: Employing financial analysis software to automate the evaluation of borrower financial statements and cash flow projections.

- **Risk Assessment Platforms**: Using risk assessment platforms that provide comprehensive borrower profiles, credit reports, and risk metrics.

- **Economic Indicators**: Monitoring economic indicators, such as unemployment rates, interest rates, and housing market trends, to gauge external risk factors.

- **Professional Networks**: Consulting with financial advisors, industry experts, and peer lenders to gain insights and share best practices for risk assessment.

Note:

A private lender subscribes to a risk assessment platform that provides real-time updates on borrower credit scores, financial health metrics, and economic indicators, helping the lender make informed decisions.

By thoroughly assessing risk and implementing effective risk management strategies, you, as a private lender, can enhance your decision-making processes, protect your investments, and achieve successful lending outcomes.

5.3 Setting Interest Rates

Setting the right interest rate is crucial for private lenders as it directly impacts the profitability of the loan and the attractiveness of the loan offer to potential borrowers. Let's explore the factors influencing interest rates, different interest rate structures, and strategies for determining appropriate rates.

1. Factors Influencing Interest Rates

Several factors influence the interest rate that a private lender might set for a loan.

- **Borrower's Creditworthiness**: The borrower's credit score and credit history significantly impact the interest rate. Higher credit scores typically result in lower interest rates, while lower scores may lead to higher rates due to increased risk.

- **Loan Amount and Term**: Larger loan amounts or longer loan terms may have different interest rates compared to smaller or shorter-term loans. Longer terms usually mean more risk for the lender, potentially leading to higher rates.

- **Collateral**: Secured loans, backed by collateral such as real estate or other valuable assets, often have lower interest rates compared to unsecured loans, as the collateral reduces the lender's risk.

- **Market Conditions**: Prevailing market interest rates, influenced by central bank policies, inflation, and overall economic conditions, affect the rates that private lenders can offer.

- **Type of Loan**: Different types of loans, such as personal loans, business loans, or real estate loans, may have varying interest rates based on their risk profiles and market demand.

- **Lender's Risk Tolerance**: The lender's own risk appetite and investment strategy also play a role in setting interest rates. A lender willing to take on higher risk might offer higher rates to compensate.

Note:

A private lender evaluating a borrower with a credit score of 750, seeking a $100,000 real estate loan for five years, would likely set a lower interest rate compared to a borrower with a score of 600 seeking an unsecured personal loan for the same amount and term.

2. Different Interest Rate Structures

Private lenders can choose from various interest rate structures when setting the terms of a loan. Understanding these structures helps tailor the loan to the specific needs of both the lender and the borrower.

- **Fixed Interest Rates**: The interest rate remains constant throughout the loan term, providing predictability for both the lender and the borrower. This structure is straightforward but may not account for changes in market conditions.

Note:

A five-year fixed-rate loan with a 6% annual interest rate ensures that the borrower pays the same interest rate for the entire duration of the loan.

- **Variable Interest Rates**: The interest rate can change over time, typically in line with a benchmark index such as the prime rate or LIBOR. Variable rates can adjust periodically, which may benefit borrowers if rates decrease, but they also carry the risk of higher payments if rates rise.

Note:

A variable-rate loan might start with a 4% interest rate, adjusting annually based on changes in the prime rate plus a margin of 2%.

- **Adjustable Interest Rates**: Similar to variable rates, adjustable rates typically start with a fixed rate for an initial period before switching to a variable rate. This can provide initial stability followed by rate adjustments based on market conditions.

Note:

An adjustable-rate mortgage (ARM) might offer a fixed 3.5% interest rate for the first five years, after which the rate adjusts annually based on the market index.

- **Interest-Only Rates**: For a certain period, the borrower pays only the interest on the loan, with the principal remaining unchanged. This structure can lower initial payments but results in higher payments later when principal repayments start.

Note:

A 10-year interest-only loan with a 5% interest rate requires the borrower to pay only the interest for the first five years, followed by higher payments that include principal repayments.

3. Strategies for Determining Interest Rates

Setting the right interest rate involves balancing competitiveness with risk and return. Here are strategies to consider:

- **Risk-Based Pricing**: Adjust interest rates based on the perceived risk of the borrower. Higher-risk borrowers receive higher rates, compensating the lender for taking on additional risk.

Note:

A private lender might offer a 5% interest rate to a borrower with excellent credit and a 10% rate to a borrower with fair credit.

- **Market Comparison**: Evaluate the interest rates offered by other lenders in the market for similar loan types and terms. Setting competitive rates can attract more borrowers while still ensuring profitability.

Note:

If the average market rate for personal loans is 8%, a private lender might offer a rate slightly lower, at 7.5%, to attract more qualified borrowers.

- **Cost of Funds**: Consider the lender's cost of capital, including borrowing costs and required return on investment. The interest rate should cover these costs and provide a satisfactory profit margin.

Note:

If a private lender's cost of capital is 4%, they might set an interest rate of 8% to cover costs and achieve a 4% profit margin.

- **Loan Terms and Conditions**: Customize the interest rate based on specific loan terms, such as shorter loan durations, lower LTV ratios, or additional borrower commitments like automatic payments.

Note:

Offering a lower interest rate of 6.5% for a short-term loan of two years, compared to 7.5% for a long-term loan of five years.

- **Economic Indicators**: Monitor economic trends and adjust interest rates accordingly. For example, in a rising interest rate environment, lenders might increase their rates to maintain margins.

Note:

If economic forecasts predict rising inflation, a private lender might preemptively increase interest rates to 9% from 8% to mitigate future cost increases.

4. Legal and Ethical Considerations

When setting interest rates, it is important to comply with legal regulations and ethical standards to avoid predatory lending practices and ensure fair treatment of borrowers.

- **Usury Laws**: These laws cap the maximum interest rate that can be charged on loans. Lenders must be aware of and comply with these limits to avoid legal repercussions.

Note:

If the state usury law caps interest rates at 12%, a private lender must set rates at or below this threshold.

- **Transparency**: Clearly disclose all terms, conditions, and costs associated with the loan to the borrower. This includes the annual percentage rate (APR), fees, and any potential rate adjustments.

Note:

Providing a comprehensive loan disclosure document that outlines the 7% fixed interest rate, associated fees, and total cost of the loan over its term.

- **Fair Lending Practices**: Ensure that interest rates and lending decisions are made without discrimination based on race, ethnicity, gender, or other protected characteristics.

Note:

Implementing standardized criteria for setting interest rates based solely on financial and credit information, ensuring fair treatment for all applicants.

By carefully considering these factors and employing thoughtful strategies, you, as a private lender, can set interest rates that are competitive, fair, and aligned with your risk tolerance and financial goals.

This balance helps attract qualified borrowers while managing risk and ensuring the profitability of the lending portfolio.

CHAPTER 6

EXAMPLES AND CASE STUDIES

6.1 Historical Case Study: J.P. Morgan

John Pierpont Morgan, commonly known as J.P. Morgan, was one of the most influential private lenders and financiers in American history. His activities in the late 19th and early 20th centuries offer valuable lessons for modern private lenders. This subchapter explores J.P. Morgan's strategies, key ventures, and the impact of his financial decisions on both the economy and the field of private lending.

1. Early Life and Career Beginnings

J.P. Morgan was born on April 17, 1837, in Hartford, Connecticut, into a wealthy banking family. His father, Junius Spencer Morgan, was a successful international banker, which provided J.P. Morgan with early exposure to the world of finance. He was educated in the U.S. and Europe, where he learned the intricacies of banking and international finance.

Key Points:

- **Education and Training**: Morgan's formal education in banking and his apprenticeship in his father's firm laid a strong foundation for his career.

- **Initial Ventures**: He began his career in 1857 at the London branch of Peabody, Morgan & Co., a firm his father co-managed. Later, he returned to the U.S. and founded J. Pierpont Morgan & Co.

2. Major Financial Ventures and Strategies

J.P. Morgan's career was marked by several key financial ventures and strategic moves that solidified his reputation as a financial titan. His strategies often involved consolidating industries, stabilizing financial markets, and providing essential capital for growth and innovation.

Key Ventures:

- **Railroad Consolidation**: Morgan played a pivotal role in reorganizing and consolidating the U.S. railroad industry. He facilitated mergers and acquisitions that created more efficient and financially stable rail networks.

Note:

Morgan orchestrated the merger of several major railroads, including the creation of the Northern Securities Company, which controlled several key railroads in the Northwest.

- **Industrial Finance**: Morgan financed and advised many of the era's largest industrial companies, including General Electric and U.S. Steel. He was instrumental in the formation of U.S. Steel in 1901, the world's first billion-dollar corporation.

Note:

The creation of the U.S. Steel involved the consolidation of Andrew Carnegie's steel operations with several other steel companies, creating a giant that dominated the industry.

- **Banking and Monetary Stability**: During financial crises, Morgan acted as a lender of last resort. His most notable intervention was during the Panic of 1907, where he organized a coalition of bankers to provide liquidity to struggling financial institutions, stabilizing the market.

Note:

Morgan's decisive action during the Panic of 1907, where he personally directed the rescue efforts from his library, helped prevent a collapse of the financial system.

3. Impact on the Economy and Private Lending

J.P. Morgan's activities had profound impacts on the U.S. economy and the development of private lending. His approach to finance and his ability to mobilize large amounts of capital had lasting effects on how private lending was conducted.

Economic Impact:

- **Industry Stabilization**: Morgan's efforts in consolidating industries and stabilizing financial markets contributed to economic stability and growth during a period of rapid industrialization and expansion in the United States.

Note:

By reorganizing failing railroads, Morgan ensured the continuous operation of a crucial industry, facilitating commerce and transportation across the nation.

- **Innovation and Growth**: His financing of new technologies and industries supported significant advancements and growth, particularly in the fields of electricity and steel production.

Note:

Private Lending Impact:

- **Risk Management**: Morgan's approach to assessing and managing risk, including his meticulous due diligence and strategic planning, set standards for modern private lending practices.

Note:

Morgan's thorough evaluation of companies before providing financing ensured that his investments were sound and minimized risk, a practice still vital in private lending today.

- **Influence on Banking Practices**: His interventions during financial crises highlighted the importance of liquidity and the role of private lenders in maintaining market stability, influencing future banking regulations and practices.

Note:

The creation of the Federal Reserve System in 1913 was partly inspired by Morgan's actions during financial panics, recognizing the need for a central bank to manage monetary stability.

4. Legacy and Lessons for Modern Private Lenders

J.P. Morgan's legacy offers several key lessons for contemporary private lenders. His strategies and decisions provide a blueprint for successful lending practices and financial management.

Lessons for Modern Private Lenders:

- **Thorough Due Diligence**: Morgan's meticulous approach to evaluating potential investments underscores the importance of thorough due diligence in mitigating risk and making informed lending decisions.

- **Diversification**: Morgan's diverse portfolio, which included railroads, industrial companies, and utilities, highlights the benefits of diversification in reducing risk and enhancing stability.

- **Crisis Management**: Morgan's leadership during financial crises demonstrates the importance of decisive action and collaboration in stabilizing markets and protecting investments.

- **Ethical Considerations**: While Morgan was a powerful financier, some of his practices raised ethical concerns, particularly regarding monopolistic behavior. Modern lenders should balance profit motives with ethical considerations and regulatory compliance.

By studying the life and career of J.P. Morgan, you can gain valuable insights into effective financial strategies, risk management practices, and the broader impact of their lending activities on the economy.

His legacy serves as both an inspiration and a cautionary tale, emphasizing the importance of innovation, diligence, and ethical considerations in private lending.

6.2 Modern Success Stories

Let's explore and examine contemporary examples of private lenders who have achieved significant success in the industry so we can identify strategies, practices, and principles that have led to their accomplishments and draw lessons for aspiring private lenders.

1. Warren Buffett and Berkshire Hathaway

Background:

Warren Buffett, the chairman and CEO of Berkshire Hathaway, is primarily known as an investor however, his activities in private lending and finance have contributed to his legendary status too.

Key Strategies:

- **Value Investing**: Buffett's approach focuses on identifying undervalued companies with strong fundamentals and long-term growth potential. He applies this principle to lending by selecting borrowers with solid financial health and promising prospects.

- **Patient Capital**: Buffett emphasizes the importance of patience in investing and lending, often holding investments for extended periods to realize their full potential.

Note:

During the 2008 financial crisis, Berkshire Hathaway provided $5 billion in capital to Goldman Sachs in exchange for preferred stock and warrants. This not only offered Goldman Sachs crucial liquidity but also secured Berkshire Hathaway a lucrative return.

Lessons Learned:

- **Thorough Research**: Buffett's success highlights the importance of thorough research and understanding the financials of potential borrowers before committing capital.

- **Long-Term Focus**: Maintaining a long-term perspective can lead to more stable and profitable lending decisions.

2. SoFi (Social Finance, Inc.)

Background:

SoFi, founded in 2011 by Stanford business school students, began as a peer-to-peer lending platform focused on student loans. It has since expanded to offer a wide range of financial products, including personal loans, mortgages, and investment services.

Key Strategies:

- **Technology and Innovation**: SoFi leverages technology to streamline the lending process, offering a user-friendly platform that simplifies loan applications and approvals.

- **Community and Networking**: SoFi built a strong community aspect by organizing events and providing career services for its members, fostering loyalty and trust.

Note:

SoFi's rapid growth is exemplified by its issuance of over $50 billion in loans and its transition to a public company in 2021. The company's innovative approach to lending has attracted a large and loyal customer base.

Lessons Learned:

- **Embrace Technology**: Utilizing advanced technology can enhance efficiency, improve customer experience, and expand the reach of lending services.

- **Build Relationships**: Creating a sense of community and offering additional value-added services can strengthen borrower relationships and loyalty.

3. LendingClub

Background:

Founded in 2007, LendingClub is one of the pioneers of online peer-to-peer lending. It connects borrowers with investors, facilitating personal loans without the traditional banking intermediaries.

Key Strategies:

- **Transparency**: LendingClub emphasizes transparency in its lending process, providing clear information on loan terms, fees, and borrower risk.

- **Risk Management**: The platform uses advanced algorithms and data analytics to assess borrower risk, ensuring that loans are appropriately priced.

Note:

LendingClub's success is reflected in its facilitation of over $60 billion in loans. Despite regulatory challenges, the company has adapted and continued to grow, showcasing resilience and innovation in the lending market.

Lessons Learned:

- **Transparency Matters**: Clear communication and transparency build trust with borrowers and investors, leading to a more reliable and reputable lending platform.

- **Data-Driven Decisions**: Leveraging data analytics can enhance risk assessment and loan pricing, improving overall lending outcomes.

4. Rocket Mortgage (Quicken Loans)

Background:

Rocket Mortgage, a subsidiary of Quicken Loans, revolutionized the mortgage industry by introducing an entirely online mortgage application process. Founded in 1985, Quicken Loans embraced digital transformation early on, leading to significant growth.

Key Strategies:

- **Digital Innovation**: Rocket Mortgage's online platform allows borrowers to apply for mortgages from their computers or mobile devices, streamlining the application process.

- **Customer Experience**: The company focuses on delivering exceptional customer service, with a strong emphasis on simplifying the borrowing process.

Note:

Rocket Mortgage became the largest mortgage lender in the United States by volume in 2018, surpassing traditional banks. Its success underscores the importance of digital innovation and customer-centric practices.

Lessons Learned:

- **Innovate Continuously**: Adopting and continually improving digital tools can set a lender apart in a competitive market.

- **Focus on Service**: Prioritizing customer experience can lead to higher satisfaction, repeat business, and positive word-of-mouth.

5. Kabbage

Background:

Kabbage, founded in 2009, provides small businesses with lines of credit through a fully automated online platform. The company uses real-time business data to make lending decisions quickly.

Key Strategies:

- **Automation and Speed**: Kabbage's platform automates the loan application and approval process, allowing small businesses to access funds rapidly.

- **Data Utilization**: By analyzing real-time business data, Kabbage can offer more accurate and timely lending decisions.

Note:

Kabbage has provided over $10 billion in funding to small businesses. Its ability to quickly assess and respond to borrower needs has made it a valuable resource for small businesses, especially during economic downturns.

Lessons Learned:

- **Speed and Efficiency**: Automating the lending process can greatly increase efficiency and borrower satisfaction.

- **Leverage Data**: Using real-time data to inform lending decisions can result in better risk management and more responsive service.

6. Marcus by Goldman Sachs

Background:

Launched in 2016, Marcus by Goldman Sachs offers personal loans and savings products directly to consumers. It represents Goldman Sachs' foray into consumer banking, leveraging its strong brand and financial expertise.

Key Strategies:

- **Brand Leverage**: Marcus benefits from the trust and reputation of Goldman Sachs, attracting customers who seek reliability and expertise.

- **Simplified Products**: Marcus offers straightforward financial products with no fees, appealing to consumers tired of complex and fee-laden banking options.

Note:

Within a few years of its launch, Marcus by Goldman Sachs had already lent billions of dollars in personal loans and attracted significant deposits, illustrating the power of brand trust and simplicity in financial products.

Lessons Learned:

- **Leverage Brand Equity**: A strong and trusted brand can attract customers and build credibility quickly.

- **Keep It Simple**: Offering simple, transparent financial products can differentiate a lender in a crowded market.

As you can see, these aspiring modern success stories can provide valuable insights into the strategies and practices that lead to success in today's lending landscape and provide a roadmap for aspiring private lenders.

There are also a few key themes that you can take from these examples, such as: embrace innovation, maintain transparency, leverage data, and prioritize customer experience.

6.3 Lessons Learned

The experiences of successful private lenders, both historical and modern, provide a wealth of knowledge for aspiring lenders.

By distilling key lessons from the stories of J.P. Morgan, Warren Buffett, SoFi, LendingClub, Rocket Mortgage, Kabbage, and Marcus by Goldman Sachs, you, as a private lender, can adopt strategies that enhance their decision-making, risk management, and overall effectiveness.

1. Thorough Due Diligence

A common thread among successful lenders is the rigorous assessment of borrowers and investment opportunities.

- **Importance:** Due diligence involves evaluating a borrower's financial health, credit history, and the viability of their proposed projects. This reduces the risk of default and ensures that the lender is making informed decisions.

- **Application:** Conduct comprehensive credit checks, financial statement analysis, and background checks. Verify the borrower's ability to repay the loan by examining their income, expenses, and existing debt.

Note:

J.P. Morgan's thorough evaluations before financing major industrial consolidations ensured that his investments were sound and minimized risk.

2. Long-Term Perspective

Successful lenders often maintain a long-term view, focusing on sustainable growth rather than short-term gains.

- **Importance:** A long-term perspective helps lenders build lasting relationships with borrowers and allows investments to mature and yield significant returns.

- **Application:** Prioritize loans and investments that promise steady, reliable returns over time. Avoid high-risk, short-term ventures that may offer quick profits but also pose substantial risks.

Note:

3. Embrace Technology

Leveraging technology is crucial in modern private lending, as it enhances efficiency and broadens access to potential borrowers.

- **Importance**: Technology can streamline the lending process, improve accuracy in risk assessment, and provide better customer experiences.

- **Application**: Invest in advanced software for loan origination, credit scoring, and data analytics. Use online platforms to reach a wider audience and automate repetitive tasks to save time and reduce errors.

Note:

4. Transparency and Ethical Practices

Building trust with borrowers and investors is essential for long-term success.

- **Importance**: Transparency in loan terms, fees, and processes fosters trust and reduces the likelihood of disputes. Ethical practices ensure compliance with regulations and promote fair treatment of borrowers.

- **Application**: Clearly communicate all aspects of the loan agreement, including interest rates, fees, and repayment schedules. Adhere to ethical standards and regulatory requirements to avoid legal issues and maintain a good reputation.

Note:

LendingClub's emphasis on transparency in its lending process builds trust with both borrowers and investors, contributing to its success.

5. Diversification

Spreading risk across different types of loans and industries can protect against downturns in any single sector.

- **Importance**: Diversification reduces the impact of a default or economic downturn in a particular industry, ensuring more stable returns.

- **Application**: Offer a variety of loan products, such as personal loans, business loans, and real estate loans. Invest in multiple sectors to mitigate the risk associated with any single borrower or industry.

Note:

J.P. Morgan's diverse portfolio, which included railroads, industrial companies, and utilities, helped stabilize his returns and reduce risk.

6. Adaptability and Innovation

The ability to adapt to changing market conditions and innovate is crucial for staying relevant and competitive.

- **Importance**: Markets and technologies evolve, and lenders who adapt quickly to these changes can capitalize on new opportunities and avoid obsolescence.

- **Application**: Stay informed about industry trends and emerging technologies. Be willing to update processes, adopt new tools, and explore novel lending products to meet changing borrower needs.

Note:

Rocket Mortgage's shift to an entirely online mortgage application process exemplifies how innovation can drive growth and capture market share.

7. Building Strong Relationships

Developing and maintaining strong relationships with borrowers, investors, and other stakeholders is key to long-term success.

- **Importance**: Strong relationships lead to repeat business, referrals, and a positive reputation. They also provide valuable insights and opportunities for collaboration.

- **Application**: Engage with borrowers through regular communication and provide exceptional customer service. Build networks with other industry professionals and investors to share knowledge and explore joint ventures.

Note:

SoFi's focus on community-building and networking has created a loyal customer base, contributing to its rapid growth and success.

8. Effective Risk Management

Identifying, assessing, and managing risk is fundamental to successful private lending.

- **Importance**: Proper risk management protects against potential losses and ensures the lender's portfolio remains healthy.

- **Application**: Implement robust risk assessment frameworks that consider credit scores, collateral value, economic conditions, and borrower behavior. Use risk mitigation techniques like requiring collateral, diversifying loan portfolios, and setting appropriate interest rates.

Note:

Warren Buffett's conservative approach to risk, which includes thorough due diligence and a preference for low-risk investments, has contributed to his enduring success.

9. Ethical Lending Practices

Maintaining high ethical standards ensures compliance with regulations and builds long-term trust with borrowers and the community.

- **Importance**: Ethical practices prevent legal issues, protect the lender's reputation, and ensure fair treatment of borrowers.

- **Application**: Adhere to all relevant laws and regulations, avoid predatory lending practices, and maintain transparency in all transactions.

Note:

Marcus by Goldman Sachs offers straightforward financial products with no fees, emphasizing transparency and fairness, which helps build customer trust and loyalty.

By incorporating these lessons into your practice, you can enhance your decision-making, improve their risk management, and ultimately achieve greater success in your lending activities.

CHAPTER 7

MANAGING YOUR LOANS

7.1 Monitoring Payments

Once a loan is issued, the work of a private lender doesn't end.

Monitoring payments is a critical part of loan management, ensuring that borrowers meet their obligations and that the lender can address issues promptly. Let's delve into the importance of monitoring payments, effective methods, tools available, and strategies to handle missed payments.

1. Importance of Monitoring Payments

- **Consistency and Cash Flow**: Regular monitoring ensures that borrowers are making payments on time, maintaining a consistent cash flow for the lender. This consistency is crucial for covering operational costs and generating profits.

- **Early Detection of Problems**: Monitoring helps detect early signs of financial trouble in borrowers. Identifying issues quickly allows the lender to take proactive steps to mitigate potential losses.

- **Maintaining Borrower Relationships**: Regular check-ins on payment status can help maintain open communication with borrowers, reinforcing the importance of timely payments and building a trustworthy relationship.

Note:

A lender who notices a borrower consistently paying late can reach out to discuss potential solutions, such as adjusting the payment schedule or offering financial advice.

2. Methods for Monitoring Payments

- **Manual Tracking**: Smaller lenders or those with few loans might manually track payments using spreadsheets or simple accounting software. This method requires regular updating and review to ensure accuracy.

- **Automated Systems**: Larger lenders or those with multiple loans typically use automated loan management systems. These systems can track payments, send reminders, and generate reports with minimal manual intervention.

- **Third-Party Services**: Some lenders outsource payment monitoring to third-party loan servicing companies. These companies handle payment tracking, collections, and even customer service on behalf of the lender.

Note:

Using an automated system, a lender can set up alerts for missed payments, ensuring they are immediately notified of any issues.

3. Tools for Monitoring Payments

- **Loan Management Software**: Tools like QuickBooks, LoanPro, and Mortgage Automator offer comprehensive solutions for tracking payments, generating reports, and managing loan portfolios.

- **Payment Gateways**: Services like PayPal, Stripe, and ACH (Automated Clearing House) facilitate seamless payment processing, ensuring timely and secure transactions.

- **Mobile Apps**: Apps specifically designed for private lenders can offer real-time payment tracking, notifications, and communication with borrowers.

Note:

A lender using LoanPro can automate payment reminders, track the payment history, and generate financial reports to monitor the overall health of their loan portfolio.

4. Strategies for Handling Missed Payments

- **Immediate Follow-Up**: As soon as a payment is missed, the lender should contact the borrower to understand the reason and discuss possible solutions. Prompt follow-up can prevent further missed payments and address any underlying issues.

- **Flexible Repayment Plans**: Offering modified repayment plans or temporary deferments can help borrowers who are experiencing short-term financial difficulties. Flexibility can help retain good borrowers and avoid defaults.

- **Late Fees and Penalties**: Clearly communicated late fees and penalties can incentivize timely payments. However, these should be used judiciously to avoid placing undue burden on borrowers.

- **Collections Process**: Establish a clear collections process for handling seriously delinquent loans. This might involve legal action, hiring a collections agency, or negotiating settlements.

Note:

If a borrower misses a payment, the lender can reach out to discuss adjusting the repayment schedule to better align with the borrower's cash flow, thereby reducing the risk of future missed payments.

5. Legal and Ethical Considerations

- **Regulatory Compliance**: Ensure all monitoring and collections practices comply with relevant laws and regulations, such as the Fair Debt Collection Practices Act (FDCPA) in the United States. Non-compliance can lead to legal issues and damage to reputation.

- **Ethical Practices**: Treat borrowers with respect and fairness, even when dealing with missed payments. Ethical practices build long-term trust and can result in better outcomes for both parties.

Note:

A lender who adheres to FDCPA guidelines during the collections process not only avoids legal repercussions but also maintains a professional and ethical relationship with borrowers.

6. Case Study: Effective Payment Monitoring

Scenario: A small private lender issues a $50,000 business loan to a local restaurant. The loan is structured with monthly payments over five years.

Implementation:

- The lender uses LoanPro for automated tracking.
- Payment reminders are set up to be sent via email and SMS five days before the due date.

- A direct debit system is implemented through ACH to facilitate automatic payments.

Outcome:

- The restaurant consistently makes payments on time, thanks to the reminders and automated payment system.

- When the restaurant owner anticipates a slow month, they inform the lender, who adjusts the payment schedule temporarily, ensuring continued payments and avoiding default.

By diligently monitoring payments, you, as a private lender, can protect your investments, maintain healthy cash flow, and foster positive relationships with borrowers.

Employing a combination of manual oversight, automated tools, and strategic responses to missed payments ensures that the lending process remains smooth and efficient.

7.2 Dealing with Late Payments

Managing late payments is a crucial aspect of loan administration.

Late payments can impact a lender's cash flow and, if not handled properly, may lead to defaults.

Let's take a look at the steps for effectively dealing with late payments, including communication strategies, potential solutions, and legal considerations.

1. Immediate Response

Importance of Prompt Action: Addressing late payments immediately helps prevent further delays and potential defaults. It also demonstrates to the borrower that the lender is vigilant and proactive.

Steps to Take:

- **Notification**: As soon as a payment is late, send a notification to the borrower. This can be an automated reminder or a personalized message. The notification should include details of the missed payment, any late fees incurred, and the urgency of resolving the issue.

- **Follow-Up Call**: If the payment remains outstanding after the initial notification, make a follow-up call. Direct communication can help understand the borrower's situation and reinforce the importance of timely payments.

Note:

A lender uses an automated system to send an email reminder on the day a payment is missed. Two days later, a follow-up call is made to discuss the issue with the borrower.

2. Understanding the Borrower's Situation

Assessment: Understanding why a payment is late is crucial for determining the appropriate response. Reasons can vary from temporary cash flow problems to more serious financial difficulties.

Questions to Ask:

- Is this a one-time issue or a recurring problem?
- What caused the delay in payment?
- When can the borrower make the payment?

Note:

A borrower explains that an unexpected medical expense caused them to miss a payment, but they can pay within a week. The lender can then decide on a short-term solution based on this information.

3. Offering Solutions

- **Flexible Repayment Plans**: Adjusting the repayment schedule or offering a short-term payment plan can help borrowers who are experiencing temporary difficulties.

- **Temporary Deferments**: In some cases, granting a deferment can provide the borrower with the necessary time to recover financially without falling further behind.

- **Waiving Late Fees**: Waiving late fees as a goodwill gesture for borrowers who typically pay on time can help maintain a positive relationship and encourage prompt future payments.

Note:

A lender offers a borrower the option to split the missed payment into two smaller payments over the next two months, making it easier for the borrower to catch up.

4. Implementing Penalties

- **Late Fees**: Implementing late fees can incentivize timely payments. However, it's important to communicate these fees clearly in the lending agreement and remind borrowers of them when payments are late.

- **Interest Rate Adjustments**: Some lenders may increase the interest rate after multiple late payments, as specified in the loan agreement. This can act as a deterrent for future late payments.

- **Legal Action**: As a last resort, pursuing legal action or involving a collections agency can be necessary for seriously delinquent accounts. This should be done in compliance with relevant laws and regulations.

Note:

A lender charges a 5% late fee for payments more than five days late. After three consecutive late payments, the lender raises the interest rate by 1%, as outlined in the loan terms.

5. Legal Considerations

- **Regulatory Compliance**: Ensure all actions taken in response to late payments comply with local, state, and federal regulations. This includes how late fees are assessed, how borrowers are contacted, and how collections are pursued.

- **Fair Debt Collection Practices**: In the United States, the Fair Debt Collection Practices Act (FDCPA) outlines specific guidelines for how lenders and collections agencies can interact with borrowers. Similar laws exist in other countries.

- **Documentation**: Keep detailed records of all communications and actions taken regarding late payments. This documentation is crucial in case of disputes or legal proceedings.

Note:

6. Maintaining Positive Relationships

- **Open Communication**: Maintaining open lines of communication with borrowers can help resolve late payments amicably. Regular check-ins and a willingness to discuss issues can foster a positive relationship.

- **Empathy and Support**: Showing empathy and offering support can encourage borrowers to be honest about their financial situations and work towards resolving payment issues.

- **Long-Term Relationship Building**: Helping a borrower through a difficult period can lead to a stronger, long-term relationship, increasing the likelihood of repeat business and positive referrals.

Note:

A lender who helps a borrower through a temporary financial setback by offering a flexible repayment plan might retain that borrower's loyalty and receive positive referrals in the future.

7. Case Study: Effective Handling of Late Payments

Scenario: A borrower misses a loan payment due to a temporary job loss.

Response:

1. **Immediate Notification**: The lender sends an automated email reminder on the due date and follows up with a phone call three days later.

2. **Understanding the Situation**: During the call, the borrower explains their job loss and expects to start a new job within a month.

3. **Offering Solutions**: The lender offers a one-month deferment and sets up a revised repayment schedule to catch up on missed payments gradually.

4. **Implementing Penalties**: Late fees are waived for this instance as a goodwill gesture.

5. **Legal Compliance**: All actions are documented, and the borrower is informed of their rights and obligations under the revised plan.

Outcome:

The borrower appreciates the lender's understanding and cooperation, successfully resumes payments after starting the new job, and remains a loyal client.

By implementing these strategies, you, as a private lender, can effectively manage late payments, mitigate risks, and maintain healthy relationships with your borrowers.

This proactive and empathetic approach not only safeguards your financial interests but also supports borrowers in overcoming temporary financial challenges.

7.3 Legal Actions

When all other efforts to resolve late payments or defaults have failed, private lenders may need to take legal action to recover the owed funds.

Let's take a look at the steps involved in pursuing legal remedies, the types of legal actions available, the process of working with attorneys and collections agencies, and the legal and ethical considerations to keep in mind.

1. When to Consider Legal Action

- **Last Resort**: Legal action should be considered only after all other attempts to resolve the issue have been exhausted, including communication, negotiation, and offering flexible repayment plans.

- **Severity of Default**: Evaluate the severity and duration of the default. Legal action is typically pursued for significant amounts or when the borrower has shown a clear inability or unwillingness to repay.

- **Cost-Benefit Analysis**: Assess the potential costs of legal action against the likelihood of successful recovery. Legal proceedings can be expensive and time-consuming, so it's essential to determine if the potential recovery justifies the effort and expense.

Note:

A lender might decide to pursue legal action after a borrower has missed multiple payments over several months and has ignored all attempts at communication and negotiation.

2. Types of Legal Actions

- **Demand Letter**: The first formal step is usually to send a demand letter, which is a written notice demanding payment of the overdue amount within a specific time frame. This letter often serves as a final warning before more serious legal action is taken.

- **Small Claims Court**: For smaller amounts, lenders can file a claim in small claims court. This is a relatively straightforward and less expensive legal avenue, though the recovery amount is typically capped based on jurisdiction limits.

- **Civil Lawsuit**: For larger sums, filing a civil lawsuit may be necessary. This involves a more formal legal process where the lender sues the borrower for breach of contract to recover the outstanding debt.

- **Secured Loan Foreclosure**: If the loan is secured by collateral (such as real estate or a vehicle), the lender can initiate foreclosure or repossession proceedings to recover the asset and sell it to recoup the loan amount.

Note:

A lender issues a demand letter to a borrower who is six months overdue on a $10,000 loan, specifying that failure to pay within 30 days will result in a lawsuit.

3. Working with Attorneys

- **Choosing the Right Attorney**: Select an attorney who specializes in debt recovery or creditor rights. Their expertise will be crucial in navigating the legal complexities and ensuring the best possible outcome.

- **Legal Fees and Costs**: Discuss the fee structure upfront, including any contingency fees, hourly rates, or flat fees. Ensure you understand all potential costs involved in the legal process.

- **Collaboration and Communication**: Maintain open lines of communication with your attorney, providing all necessary documentation and background information about the loan and the borrower. Regular updates on the case progress are essential.

Note:

A lender hires a debt recovery attorney on a contingency fee basis, where the attorney receives a percentage of the recovered amount, minimizing upfront costs for the lender.

4. Collections Agencies

- **When to Use Collections Agencies**: For delinquent loans that are difficult to recover, using a collections agency can be a viable option. Collections agencies specialize in recovering debts and have the resources and expertise to pursue debtors effectively.

- **Agency Selection**: Choose a reputable collections agency with experience in your specific type of loan and borrower demographic. Verify their compliance with relevant regulations and their success rate in recovering debts.

- **Fee Structures**: Collections agencies typically charge a percentage of the recovered amount as their fee. Ensure you understand the fee structure and any additional costs that may apply.

- **Ethical Considerations**: Ensure the agency follows ethical practices and complies with all regulations, such as the Fair Debt Collection Practices Act (FDCPA) in the United States, to avoid legal issues and maintain your reputation.

Note:

A lender contracts a collections agency to recover a $5,000 delinquent loan, agreeing to a 25% contingency fee. The agency successfully recovers the debt, and the lender receives $3,750.

5. Legal and Ethical Considerations

- **Regulatory Compliance**: Ensure that all legal actions comply with local, state, and federal laws. Non-compliance can lead to legal penalties and damage to your reputation.
- **Fair Treatment**: Treat borrowers fairly and respectfully throughout the legal process. Ethical treatment can preserve your reputation and potentially lead to more cooperative resolution of the debt.
- **Documentation**: Keep detailed records of all communications, legal actions, and payments related to the delinquent loan. Thorough documentation is essential for legal proceedings and defending against potential counterclaims.

Note:

A lender ensures all actions taken against a defaulting borrower comply with the FDCPA, avoiding aggressive tactics and maintaining detailed records of all communications and legal steps.

6. Case Study: Successful Legal Action

Scenario: A lender issues a $20,000 business loan secured by equipment. The borrower defaults, and all attempts at negotiation fail.

Steps Taken:

1. **Demand Letter**: A demand letter is sent, giving the borrower 30 days to pay the overdue amount.

2. **Foreclosure Proceedings**: When the borrower fails to respond, the lender initiates foreclosure on the equipment.

3. **Legal Action**: The lender files a civil lawsuit to recover any remaining unpaid amount after the equipment is sold.

Outcome:

The lender successfully repossesses and sells the equipment for $15,000, reducing the outstanding debt to $5,000. The civil lawsuit results in a judgment for the remaining amount, which the borrower is ordered to pay over time.

By understanding and effectively utilizing legal actions, you, as a private lender, can protect your investments and maximize recovery of delinquent loans.

While legal action is a last resort, it is an essential tool in the private lender's arsenal, ensuring that borrowers meet their obligations and that lenders can mitigate potential losses.

CHAPTER 8

GROWING YOUR PRIVATE LENDING BUSINESS

8.1 Reinvesting Profits

Reinvesting profits is a critical strategy for growing your private lending business.

By wisely allocating the earnings from your lending activities, you can increase your capital base, diversify your loan portfolio, enhance operational efficiencies, and ultimately achieve sustainable growth.

1. Increasing Your Capital Base

- **Retained Earnings**: Retaining a portion of your profits within the business increases the funds available for future lending. This approach strengthens your financial position and enables you to issue larger or more loans.

- **Capital Reserves**: Building a capital reserve can provide a safety net for your business, ensuring you have funds available to cover unexpected losses or seize new opportunities.

Note:

A lender who retains 30% of their annual profits can gradually build a substantial fund, allowing for larger loans or investment in new opportunities without needing to secure additional external financing.

2. Expanding Your Loan Portfolio

- **Diversification**: Use profits to diversify your loan portfolio by entering new markets or offering different types of loans. This can spread risk and reduce dependence on a single market segment.

- **New Loan Products**: Introducing new loan products, such as secured loans, business loans, or real estate loans, can attract a broader range of borrowers and increase your revenue streams.

- **Geographical Expansion**: Expanding into new geographic regions can open up additional markets and reduce exposure to local economic downturns.

Note:

A lender specializing in personal loans uses profits to enter the small business loan market, thereby diversifying their portfolio and tapping into a new customer base.

3. Investing in Technology

- **Loan Management Software**: Invest in advanced loan management systems to automate and streamline your operations. This can improve efficiency, reduce errors, and provide better service to borrowers.

- **Data Analytics**: Utilize data analytics tools to gain insights into borrower behavior, market trends, and risk factors. This information can guide your lending decisions and enhance risk management.

- **Customer Experience**: Improve the borrower experience by investing in user-friendly online platforms and mobile apps that simplify the application process and provide easy access to account information.

Note:

A lender invests in a state-of-the-art loan management system that automates payment tracking and generates real-time reports, freeing up time for strategic decision-making.

4. Enhancing Your Expertise

- **Professional Development**: Allocate funds for ongoing education and training. This can include attending industry conferences, enrolling in financial courses, and obtaining relevant certifications.

- **Advisory Services**: Hire financial advisors or consultants to provide expert guidance on complex lending decisions, portfolio management, and business strategy.

- **Networking**: Join industry associations and networks to stay informed about the latest trends, regulations, and best practices in private lending.

Note:

A lender attends a series of workshops on advanced credit risk assessment techniques, gaining valuable knowledge that improves their lending practices and decision-making process.

5. Marketing and Business Development

- **Brand Building**: Use profits to build and strengthen your brand through marketing campaigns, social media presence, and professional websites. A strong brand can attract more borrowers and investors.

- **Client Acquisition**: Invest in strategies to acquire new clients, such as targeted advertising, referral programs, and partnerships with real estate agents or financial advisors.

- **Customer Retention**: Develop customer loyalty programs and offer incentives for repeat business, fostering long-term relationships with borrowers.

Note:

A lender launches a targeted online marketing campaign to attract real estate investors, resulting in an increase in loan applications from this segment.

6. Building Strategic Partnerships

- **Collaborations**: Form partnerships with other financial institutions, real estate firms, or businesses to expand your reach and offer complementary services.

- **Joint Ventures**: Engage in joint ventures with other private lenders to share risks and benefits, enabling you to undertake larger projects or enter new markets.

Note:

A private lender partners with a local real estate firm to offer specialized loans to homebuyers, leveraging the firm's market knowledge and client base.

7. Risk Management

- **Insurance**: Invest in insurance products to protect your business against potential losses from borrower defaults, legal issues, or operational risks.

- **Reserves for Bad Debt**: Allocate a portion of profits to create a reserve fund specifically for covering bad debts. This fund can provide a buffer against unexpected losses and maintain financial stability.

Note:

A lender sets aside 5% of annual profits to build a reserve for bad debt, ensuring they can absorb losses from unforeseen borrower defaults without compromising their financial health.

8. Scaling Operations

- **Hiring Staff**: As your business grows, reinvest profits in hiring additional staff to manage increased workloads and expand your operations. This includes loan officers, risk analysts, and customer service representatives.

- **Office Expansion**: If necessary, invest in larger or additional office spaces to accommodate your growing team and improve operational efficiency.

Note:

A lender experiencing rapid growth hires two new loan officers and a risk analyst, allowing them to process more applications and better manage risk.

Enhance your business capabilities, reduce risks, and position yourself for long-term success by strategically reinvesting profits.

8.2 Networking

Networking is a fundamental strategy for growing your private lending business.

By building relationships with industry peers, professionals, and potential borrowers, you can access new opportunities, gain valuable insights, and enhance your reputation.

1. Importance of Networking

- **Access to Opportunities**: Networking opens doors to new opportunities, including potential borrowers, strategic partnerships, and investment opportunities. By expanding your professional network, you increase your chances of finding lucrative deals and expanding your business.

- **Industry Insights**: Networking allows you to stay informed about industry trends, market conditions, and regulatory changes. Engaging with peers and experts provides valuable insights that can inform your lending decisions and business strategies.

- **Building Trust and Reputation**: Establishing meaningful connections within the industry helps build trust and credibility for your lending business. A positive reputation can attract borrowers and investors and lead to referrals and repeat business.

Note:

Attending a networking event allows a private lender to meet a real estate developer who is looking for financing for an upcoming project. This connection leads to a profitable loan opportunity and establishes the lender as a reliable partner in the developer's network.

2. Effective Networking Strategies

- **Attend Industry Events**: Attend conferences, seminars, and networking events specifically targeted at the private lending industry. These events provide opportunities to meet industry professionals, learn from experts, and showcase your expertise.

- **Join Professional Associations**: Join industry associations and organizations related to private lending, such as the American Association of Private Lenders (AAPL) or the National Private Lenders Association (NPLA). Membership offers networking opportunities, educational resources, and industry recognition.

- **Utilize Online Platforms**: Participate in online forums, social media groups, and professional networking platforms like LinkedIn. Engage in discussions, share insights, and connect with other professionals in the private lending industry.

- **Build Personal Relationships**: Networking is about building genuine relationships, so focus on establishing rapport and trust with your contacts. Take the time to understand their needs and interests, and offer support and assistance when possible.

Note:

A private lender attends a real estate investment conference and connects with several investors and property developers. By actively participating in discussions and sharing expertise, the lender builds strong relationships that lead to future loan opportunities.

3. Benefits of Networking

- **Access to Deal Flow**: Networking expands your access to deal flow, allowing you to identify potential lending opportunities that you might not have discovered otherwise. By leveraging your network, you can tap into a broader pool of borrowers and investment opportunities.

- **Referrals and Recommendations**: A strong network can generate referrals and recommendations from industry peers, professionals, and satisfied clients. Positive word-of-mouth can significantly enhance your reputation and credibility, attracting new borrowers and investors to your business.

- **Collaborative Opportunities**: Networking facilitates collaboration with other industry professionals, such as real estate agents, attorneys, and financial advisors. These collaborations can lead to mutually beneficial partnerships, joint ventures, and co-investment opportunities.

Note:

Through networking, a private lender establishes a referral partnership with a real estate brokerage firm. The firm refers clients in need of financing to the lender, and in return, the lender refers borrowers seeking properties to the brokerage firm, creating a symbiotic relationship.

4. Building Your Network

- **Identify Key Contacts**: Identify key contacts within the private lending industry, including other lenders, investors, real estate professionals, and legal experts. These contacts can provide valuable insights, referrals, and collaboration opportunities.

- **Attend Networking Events**: Actively participate in networking events, both in-person and online. Look for events specifically tailored to the private lending industry, as well as broader real estate and finance events where you can meet potential borrowers and partners.

- **Follow Up and Nurture Relationships**: After making initial connections, follow up with your contacts to maintain the relationship. Keep in touch through email, phone calls, or social media, and offer assistance or support whenever possible.

- **Provide Value**: Networking is a two-way street, so look for ways to provide value to your contacts. Share industry insights, offer referrals, or provide assistance with their projects or initiatives. By giving value first, you build goodwill and strengthen your relationships.

Note:

A private lender follows up with contacts made at a networking event by sending personalized emails thanking them for the conversation and offering to connect further over coffee or a phone call to discuss potential collaboration opportunities.

5. Leveraging Your Network

- **Seek Advice and Guidance**: Don't hesitate to reach out to your network for advice, guidance, or mentorship. Experienced industry professionals can offer valuable insights and perspectives that can help you navigate challenges and make informed decisions.

- **Collaborate on Projects**: Look for opportunities to collaborate with your network on projects, joint ventures, or co-investment opportunities. By pooling resources and expertise, you can undertake larger and more profitable deals.

- **Stay Engaged and Active**: Continuously nurture and expand your network by staying engaged and active within the industry. Attend networking events regularly, participate in online discussions, and seek out new connections to maintain momentum and foster growth.

Note:

A private lender leverages their network to collaborate with a real estate developer on a large-scale project. By combining their financing expertise with the developer's industry knowledge, they successfully fund and complete the project, generating significant returns for both parties.

By investing time and effort into building and nurturing relationships within the industry, you can access new opportunities, gain valuable insights, and establish yourself as a trusted and respected lender.

Continuously expand and leverage your network to position yourself for long-term success and sustainable growth in the competitive private lending market.

8.3 Diversifying Your Portfolio

Diversifying your loan portfolio is a strategic approach to growing your private lending business while mitigating risks.

By spreading your investments across different types of loans, borrowers, and industries, you can reduce the impact of potential losses and capitalize on various opportunities.

1. Importance of Portfolio Diversification

- **Risk Management**: Diversification helps mitigate risks by reducing the impact of any single loan default or economic downturn. A well-diversified portfolio is less vulnerable to market fluctuations and borrower-specific issues.

- **Enhanced Stability**: A diversified portfolio provides stability and consistency in returns over time. While some loans may underperform, others may outperform, resulting in a more predictable overall performance.

- **Optimized Returns**: By allocating investments across different asset classes and loan types, you can optimize returns by balancing risk and reward. Diversification allows you to capture opportunities in various market segments and maximize your overall profitability.

Note:

A private lender who diversifies their portfolio across personal loans, real estate loans, and business loans is better positioned to withstand economic downturns or sector-specific challenges, ensuring more stable returns over time.

2. Effective Diversification Strategies

- **Asset Class Diversification**: Allocate investments across different asset classes, such as consumer loans, real estate loans, small business loans, and commercial loans. Each asset class has its own risk-return profile, allowing you to balance risk across your portfolio.

- **Geographic Diversification**: Spread your loans across different geographic regions to reduce exposure to localized economic risks. Investing in diverse markets can provide a buffer against regional economic downturns or regulatory changes.

- **Borrower Profile Diversification**: Cater to a diverse range of borrowers, including individuals, small businesses, real estate investors, and established corporations. Each borrower segment has its own credit risk characteristics, diversifying your exposure to borrower-specific risks.

- **Loan Term Diversification**: Invest in loans with varying maturity periods, ranging from short-term bridge loans to long-term installment loans. Diversifying loan terms helps manage liquidity risk and ensures a steady stream of cash flow over time.

Note:

A private lender diversifies their portfolio by investing in a mix of short-term real estate bridge loans, medium-term business expansion loans, and long-term personal installment loans, effectively spreading risk across different loan types and durations.

3. Benefits of Portfolio Diversification

- **Risk Reduction**: Portfolio diversification reduces the overall risk of your lending business by spreading investments across multiple assets and borrowers. Even if some loans default, the impact on your portfolio is minimized, preserving your capital and profitability.

- **Enhanced Flexibility**: A diversified portfolio provides flexibility to adapt to changing market conditions and borrower preferences. You can adjust your investment allocations based on emerging opportunities or shifting risk factors, ensuring agility and responsiveness in your lending strategy.

- **Stable Returns**: Diversification leads to more stable and consistent returns over time, as losses from underperforming loans are offset by gains from well-performing loans. This balanced approach helps smooth out volatility and uncertainty in your investment portfolio.

Note:

During an economic downturn, a private lender with a diversified portfolio experiences lower overall losses compared to a lender heavily concentrated in a single asset class or market segment. The diversified lender's exposure to different industries and borrower profiles provides resilience against adverse market conditions.

4. Implementation of Portfolio Diversification

- **Risk Assessment**: Conduct thorough risk assessments of potential loans before investing. Evaluate factors such as borrower creditworthiness, collateral quality, market conditions, and economic outlook to identify potential risks and opportunities.

- **Portfolio Allocation**: Allocate investments strategically across different asset classes, geographic regions, and borrower segments based on your risk tolerance and investment objectives. Maintain a balanced portfolio mix that optimizes risk-return dynamics and aligns with your long-term goals.

- **Continuous Monitoring**: Regularly monitor and review your loan portfolio to assess performance, identify emerging risks, and make necessary adjustments. Rebalance your portfolio periodically to ensure it remains diversified and aligned with your investment strategy.

Note:

A private lender utilizes advanced risk assessment tools and analytics to evaluate loan opportunities and allocate investments across their portfolio. They conduct regular portfolio reviews to track performance metrics, identify areas for improvement, and optimize their diversification strategy based on evolving market conditions.

5. Leveraging Technology and Data Analytics

- **Advanced Tools**: Utilize technology-driven loan management systems and data analytics platforms to streamline portfolio management processes and gain actionable insights into portfolio performance.

- **Risk Modeling**: Implement sophisticated risk modeling techniques to assess and quantify portfolio risks, identify correlations between different assets, and optimize portfolio diversification strategies.

- **Predictive Analytics**: Leverage predictive analytics and machine learning algorithms to forecast loan defaults, estimate potential losses, and proactively manage risk exposure across your portfolio.

Note:

A private lender adopts a state-of-the-art loan management platform equipped with predictive analytics capabilities. By analyzing historical loan data and macroeconomic indicators, they develop predictive models that accurately forecast default probabilities and guide portfolio diversification decisions.

6. Case Study: Successful Portfolio Diversification

Scenario: A private lender diversifies their loan portfolio by investing in a mix of real estate loans, business loans, and personal loans across different geographic regions.

Implementation:

1. **Asset Class Diversification**: The lender allocates investments across residential mortgages, commercial real estate loans, small business loans, and consumer installment loans.

2. **Geographic Diversification**: Loans originate in diverse markets, including urban, suburban, and rural areas across multiple states.

3. **Borrower Profile Diversification**: The lender caters to a broad spectrum of borrowers, including individual homebuyers, real estate investors, small business owners, and creditworthy consumers.

4. **Loan Term Diversification**: Investments are spread across short-term bridge loans, medium-term commercial mortgages, and long-term personal installment loans to manage liquidity risk and optimize cash flow.

Outcome:

The lender's diversified portfolio delivers stable and consistent returns over time, with minimal losses even during periods of economic uncertainty. By spreading risk across different asset classes and borrower segments, the lender achieves long-term profitability and resilience against market volatility.

By adopting effective diversification strategies, leveraging technology and data analytics, and continuously monitoring and adjusting your portfolio, you can optimize risk-adjusted returns and position your lending business for sustainable growth and resilience in dynamic market environments.

CHAPTER 9

PASSIVE LENDING OPTIONS

9.1 Peer-to-Peer Lending Platforms

Peer-to-peer (P2P) lending platforms offer passive lending options for private lenders seeking to diversify their investment portfolios and earn passive income.

These platforms connect individual lenders with borrowers through online marketplaces, facilitating loan origination, servicing, and repayment.

Let's explore the benefits of P2P lending platforms, key considerations for private lenders, and strategies for maximizing returns.

1. Understanding Peer-to-Peer Lending

- **Marketplace Model**: P2P lending platforms operate as online marketplaces where individual investors (lenders) can directly fund loans for individual borrowers. The platform facilitates the loan origination process, including borrower screening, loan underwriting, and documentation.

- **Diverse Borrower Base**: P2P lending platforms attract a diverse range of borrowers, including individuals, small businesses, and real estate investors. Borrowers may seek financing for various purposes, such as debt consolidation, home improvement, or business expansion.

- **Risk and Return**: P2P lending offers the potential for attractive returns compared to traditional investment options like savings accounts or bonds. However, it also carries inherent risks, including borrower default, platform risk, and economic downturns.

Note:

A private lender invests $10,000 in a P2P lending platform, funding loans to multiple borrowers with varying credit profiles and loan purposes. Over time, the lender earns interest income and receives principal repayments as borrowers fulfill their loan obligations.

2. Benefits of Peer-to-Peer Lending Platforms

- **Diversification**: P2P lending platforms allow private lenders to diversify their investment portfolios by spreading investments across multiple loans and borrowers. This diversification helps mitigate individual loan default risk and enhances overall portfolio stability.

- **Passive Income**: P2P lending offers passive income opportunities, allowing lenders to earn interest income without actively managing individual loans. Once funds are invested, lenders can enjoy regular interest payments and principal repayments over the loan term.

- **Accessibility**: P2P lending platforms provide accessible investment opportunities for individual lenders, with low minimum investment requirements and user-friendly online interfaces. Lenders can easily browse available loan listings, review borrower profiles, and make investment decisions based on their preferences.

Note:

A private lender with limited time and resources to actively manage loans appreciates the passive income potential of P2P lending platforms. By investing in a diversified portfolio of loans, the lender earns regular interest payments without the need for daily monitoring or administration.

3. Key Considerations for Private Lenders

- **Risk Assessment**: Conduct thorough due diligence before investing in P2P loans, including assessing borrower creditworthiness, loan terms, and platform reputation. Evaluate factors such as borrower credit scores, income stability, and loan purpose to gauge risk levels.

- **Platform Selection**: Choose reputable P2P lending platforms with a track record of success, transparent fee structures, and robust risk management practices. Research platform reviews, borrower feedback, and historical performance data to make informed investment decisions.

- **Diversification Strategy**: Implement a diversified investment strategy by spreading investments across multiple loans, borrowers, and loan grades. Avoid concentrating too much capital in a single loan or borrower, as this increases exposure to individual default risk.

Note:

A private lender interested in investing in P2P loans conducts thorough research on multiple platforms, comparing loan offerings, borrower demographics, and historical performance metrics. After selecting reputable platforms with favorable risk-return profiles, the lender diversifies investments across various loan grades and terms to minimize risk.

4. Maximizing Returns on Peer-to-Peer Lending Investments

- **Portfolio Monitoring**: Regularly monitor the performance of your P2P lending portfolio, including tracking loan repayments, assessing borrower defaults, and adjusting investment allocations as needed. Stay on top of the economic trends, platform updates, and regulatory changes that may impact your investments.

- **Reinvestment Strategy**: Reinvest interest income and principal repayments from matured loans into new loan opportunities to compound returns over time. Implement a disciplined reinvestment strategy based on your risk tolerance, liquidity needs, and investment objectives.

- **Risk Management**: Continuously assess and manage risk within your P2P lending portfolio, including diversifying investments, setting risk limits, and adjusting investment allocations based on changing market conditions. Stay vigilant for early warning signs of potential borrower defaults or platform instability.

Note:

A private lender regularly reviews their P2P lending portfolio performance using platform dashboards and investment tracking tools. When a loan matures and generates principal repayment, the lender reinvests the proceeds into new loan opportunities with similar risk-return profiles, optimizing portfolio returns and maintaining diversification.

5. Case Study: Successful P2P Lending Portfolio

Scenario: A private lender invests $20,000 in a P2P lending platform and diversifies their portfolio across multiple loans and loan grades.

Implementation:

1. **Risk Assessment**: The lender conducts thorough due diligence on borrower profiles, loan terms, and platform performance metrics before investing.

2. **Diversification Strategy**: Investments are spread across different loan grades, loan purposes, and borrower demographics to minimize individual default risk.

3. **Portfolio Monitoring**: The lender regularly monitors loan performance, tracks interest payments and principal repayments, and adjusts investment allocations based on evolving risk factors.

4. **Reinvestment Strategy**: Interest income and principal repayments from matured loans are reinvested into new loan opportunities to compound returns and maintain portfolio diversification.

Outcome:

The lender's disciplined approach to P2P lending investment results in steady interest income and principal repayments over time. By diversifying investments and actively managing their portfolio, the lender achieves attractive risk-adjusted returns and mitigates the impact of individual loan defaults.

Peer-to-peer lending platforms offer private lenders a passive investment option to diversify their portfolios and earn attractive returns.

If you conduct thorough due diligence, diversify investments, and implement disciplined portfolio management strategies, you can maximize the benefits of P2P lending while managing risks effectively.

9.2 Investing in Private Lending Funds

Investing in private lending funds provides passive lending options for individuals seeking exposure to the private lending market without the need for active loan management.

These funds pool capital from multiple investors to fund a diversified portfolio of loans, managed by professional fund managers.

Let's explore the benefits of private lending funds, key considerations for investors, and strategies for maximizing returns.

1. Understanding Private Lending Funds

- **Fund Structure**: Private lending funds operate as pooled investment vehicles that aggregate capital from multiple investors to deploy in a portfolio of loans. The fund manager is responsible for sourcing, underwriting, and managing the loans on behalf of investors.

- **Diversification**: Private lending funds offer diversification benefits by investing in a wide range of loans across different asset classes, industries, and geographic regions. By doing so, it helps spread risk and enhance portfolio stability.

- **Professional Management**: Fund managers leverage their expertise and experience to identify attractive loan opportunities, conduct due diligence, and manage loan portfolios effectively. Investors benefit from the expertise of seasoned professionals without the need for hands-on involvement.

Note:

An investor allocates $50,000 to a private lending fund focused on real estate bridge loans. The fund manager deploys the capital across a diversified portfolio of short-term loans secured by residential and commercial properties, generating regular interest income for the investor.

2. Benefits of Private Lending Funds

- **Passive Income**: Private lending funds offer passive income opportunities for investors, allowing them to earn regular interest payments without actively managing individual loans. Once invested, investors can enjoy cash flow from interest income and principal repayments.

- **Professional Management**: Investors benefit from the expertise and resources of professional fund managers who specialize in private lending. Fund managers handle all aspects of loan origination, underwriting, and servicing, relieving investors of the administrative burden.

- **Diversification**: Private lending funds provide diversification benefits by investing in a portfolio of loans across different sectors, borrowers, and risk profiles. This diversification helps reduce individual loan default risk and enhances overall portfolio stability.

Note:

An investor seeking passive income and portfolio diversification allocates a portion of their investment portfolio to a private lending fund. By leveraging the expertise of the fund manager and accessing a diversified portfolio of loans, the investor achieves consistent returns with reduced risk.

3. Key Considerations for Investors

- **Risk Assessment**: Conduct due diligence on the private lending fund, including reviewing the fund's investment strategy, track record, and performance metrics. Assess factors such as loan underwriting standards, borrower credit quality, and portfolio diversification.

- **Manager Reputation**: Evaluate the reputation and experience of the fund manager, including their track record in private lending, investment philosophy, and risk management practices. Choose fund managers with a proven track record of success and integrity.

- **Fee Structure**: Understand the fee structure of the private lending fund, including management fees, performance fees, and other expenses. Evaluate the impact of fees on overall returns and ensure alignment with your investment objectives.

- **Liquidity Considerations**: Consider the liquidity terms of the private lending fund, including redemption policies, lock-up periods, and exit strategies. Assess your liquidity needs and investment horizon to ensure compatibility with the fund's structure.

Note:

An investor interested in private lending funds researches multiple fund options, comparing investment strategies, fee structures, and manager credentials. After conducting thorough due diligence and assessing their risk tolerance and investment goals, the investor selects a reputable fund with a diversified loan portfolio and transparent fee arrangements.

4. Maximizing Returns on Private Lending Fund Investments

- **Portfolio Monitoring**: Stay informed about the performance of the private lending fund by reviewing regular performance reports, loan updates, and manager communications. Monitor key performance metrics such as loan delinquencies, default rates, and portfolio composition.

- **Diversification Strategy**: Seek opportunities to diversify your investment portfolio by allocating capital to multiple private lending funds with complementary strategies and risk profiles. Diversification helps spread risk and enhance overall portfolio resilience.

- **Reinvestment Strategy**: Reinvest distributions and dividends from private lending funds to compound returns over time. Consider reinvesting proceeds into additional fund investments or other income-generating opportunities to maximize long-term growth potential.

Note:

An investor regularly reviews performance reports and updates from their private lending fund manager, tracking loan performance and portfolio metrics. When distributions are received, the investor reinvests the proceeds into additional fund shares to compound returns and capitalize on investment opportunities.

5. Case Study: Successful Private Lending Fund Investment

Scenario: An investor allocates $100,000 to a private lending fund focused on small business loans.

Implementation:

1. **Due Diligence**: The investor conducts thorough due diligence on the fund's investment strategy, manager expertise, and track record. After reviewing performance metrics and assessing risk factors, the investor decides to invest in the fund.

2. **Portfolio Diversification**: The fund manager deploys the investor's capital across a diversified portfolio of small business loans, including various industries and geographic regions.

3. **Performance Monitoring**: The investor regularly monitors fund performance through performance reports, manager updates, and investor communications. Key metrics such as loan default rates, delinquencies, and interest income are tracked.

4. **Reinvestment Strategy**: Distributions and dividends received from the fund are reinvested to compound returns over time. The investor evaluates opportunities to reinvest proceeds into additional fund shares or other income-generating investments.

Outcome:

The investor's investment in the private lending fund generates consistent income through regular interest payments and distributions. By leveraging the expertise of the fund manager and accessing a diversified portfolio of small business loans, the investor achieves attractive risk-adjusted returns and portfolio diversification.

Investing in private lending funds offers passive income opportunities and portfolio diversification benefits for investors seeking exposure to the private lending market.

By conducting thorough due diligence, selecting reputable fund managers, and implementing disciplined investment strategies, you, as an investor and private money lender, can maximize returns and manage risk effectively in the dynamic private lending landscape.

If you like the idea of investing in private lending FUND, feel free to explore opportunities with our Y2 Capital Group Debt Fund. You can check us out at https://y2lending.com/invest

9.3 Becoming a Silent Partner

Becoming a silent partner in a lending venture is a passive lending option that allows individuals to invest capital in lending activities without actively participating in loan origination, management, or decision-making.

As a silent partner, investors provide funding to lending businesses or platforms in exchange for a share of the profits generated from loan investments.

Let's explore the concept of silent partnership in lending, its benefits, considerations for investors, and strategies for maximizing returns.

1. Understanding Silent Partnership

- **Passive Investment**: Silent partnership involves providing capital to lending businesses or platforms as an investor without taking an active role in day-to-day operations or decision-making. Investors contribute funds to finance loan activities and share in the profits generated from loan investments.

- **Profit Sharing**: Silent partners receive a portion of the profits earned by the lending business or platform based on the terms of the partnership agreement. Profit-sharing arrangements may vary depending on factors such as investment size, risk profile, and expected returns.

- **Limited Involvement**: Silent partners do not participate in the management, underwriting, or servicing of loans. They entrust the lending business or platform to handle all aspects of loan origination, administration, and collections on their behalf.

Note:

An investor becomes a silent partner in a real estate lending firm, providing $100,000 in capital to finance property loans. In exchange for their investment, the investor receives a share of the profits generated from interest income and loan repayments.

2. Benefits of Silent Partnership

- **Passive Income**: Silent partnership offers passive income opportunities for investors, allowing them to earn returns on their investment without actively managing loan activities. Investors can enjoy regular cash flow from interest payments and loan repayments.

- **Risk Mitigation**: Silent partners share the risks and rewards of lending activities with the lending business or platform. By diversifying investments across multiple loans and borrowers, investors can mitigate individual loan default risk and enhance portfolio stability.

- **Limited Liability**: Silent partners typically have limited liability for the obligations and liabilities of the lending business or platform. Their financial exposure is limited to the amount of capital invested, reducing personal risk in the event of loan defaults or business losses.

Note:

An investor seeking passive income and portfolio diversification becomes a silent partner in a lending platform specializing in consumer loans. By investing capital in the platform, the investor earns regular returns from interest income and benefits from risk-sharing with the platform.

3. Considerations for Silent Partners

- **Partnership Agreement**: Review the terms of the partnership agreement carefully, including profit-sharing arrangements, investment terms, and exit options. Ensure that the agreement outlines the rights and responsibilities of both parties and addresses key considerations such as capital contributions, distributions, and dispute resolution.

- **Due Diligence**: Conduct due diligence on the lending business or platform before entering into a silent partnership. Evaluate factors such as the business model, track record, regulatory compliance, and risk management practices to assess the viability and reputation of the partner.

- **Risk Assessment**: Assess the risks associated with the lending activities undertaken by the partner, including borrower credit risk, market risk, and operational risk. Consider factors such as loan underwriting standards, portfolio diversification, and contingency plans for managing adverse scenarios.

Note:

An investor interested in becoming a silent partner in a lending venture conducts thorough due diligence on the partner's business model, loan portfolio, and regulatory compliance. After reviewing the partnership agreement and assessing risk factors, the investor decides to proceed with the investment.

4. Maximizing Returns as a Silent Partner

- **Diversification Strategy**: Consider diversifying investments across multiple silent partnerships to spread risk and enhance portfolio resilience. Allocate capital to partners with complementary strategies, geographic focus, and risk profiles to achieve balanced exposure.

- **Regular Monitoring**: Stay informed about the performance of your silent partnerships by monitoring financial reports, investment updates, and key performance metrics. Regular communication with partners helps ensure transparency and accountability in partnership activities.

- **Reinvestment Strategy**: Reinvest profits and distributions from silent partnerships to compound returns over time. Evaluate opportunities to reinvest proceeds into additional partnerships or other income-generating investments to maximize long-term growth potential.

Note:

An investor diversifies their portfolio by becoming a silent partner in multiple lending ventures, including real estate lending, small business lending, and consumer lending. By regularly monitoring partnership performance and reinvesting profits, the investor achieves attractive returns and portfolio diversification.

5. Case Study: Successful Silent Partnership

Scenario: An investor becomes a silent partner in a lending platform specializing in small business loans.

Implementation:

1. **Partnership Agreement**: The investor reviews the partnership agreement, which outlines profit-sharing arrangements, investment terms, and governance structure.

2. **Due Diligence**: Thorough due diligence is conducted on the lending platform, including reviewing loan portfolios, platform performance, and regulatory compliance.

3. **Capital Investment**: The investor commits $50,000 in capital to the partnership, in exchange for a share of the profits generated from loan investments.

4. **Regular Monitoring**: The investor monitors partnership performance through financial reports, investment updates, and quarterly meetings with the platform management team.

5. **Reinvestment Strategy**: Profits and distributions received from the partnership are reinvested to compound returns over time, with a focus on portfolio diversification and risk management.

Outcome:

The investor's silent partnership in the lending platform generates consistent income through regular interest payments and profit distributions. By leveraging the expertise of the platform management team and sharing in the risks and rewards of lending activities, the investor achieves attractive risk-adjusted returns and portfolio diversification.

Becoming a silent partner in a lending venture offers passive income opportunities and portfolio diversification benefits for investors seeking exposure to the lending market.

Review partnership agreements, conduct due diligence, and implement disciplined investment strategies, and you, as a silent partner, can maximize returns and manage risks effectively in the dynamic lending landscape.

If you like the idea of investing as a silent partner, feel free to explore opportunities with our Y2 Capital Group Debt Fund. You can check us out at https://y2lending.com/invest

CHAPTER 10

COMMON PITFALLS AND HOW TO AVOID THEM

10.1 Scams and Fraud

Scams and fraud are prevalent risks in the private lending industry, posing significant threats to investors' capital and financial well-being.

Understanding common scams and fraud schemes can help investors identify red flags and protect themselves from potential losses.

Let's explore various types of scams and fraud in private lending, warning signs to watch out for, and strategies to avoid falling victim to fraudulent activities.

1. Types of Scams and Fraud

- **Phantom Loans**: Fraudulent lenders offer nonexistent loans or investment opportunities to unsuspecting investors. These phantom loans often promise high returns with minimal risk but are designed to deceive investors into providing upfront fees or personal information without receiving any legitimate financing.

- **Advance Fee Fraud**: Scammers request upfront fees from borrowers or investors under the guise of processing fees, loan origination fees, or insurance premiums. Once the fees are paid, the scammer disappears without providing the promised loan or investment, leaving victims with financial losses.

- **Identity Theft**: Fraudsters may steal personal or financial information from investors or borrowers to commit identity theft. This information can be used to open fraudulent accounts, apply for loans, or engage in other illegal activities, causing financial harm and reputational damage to victims.

- **Ponzi Schemes**: Ponzi schemes involve using funds from new investors to pay returns to earlier investors, creating the illusion of profitability. As the scheme relies on a continuous influx of new capital to sustain payouts, it inevitably collapses when new investments dry up, resulting in substantial losses for investors.

Note:

An investor receives an unsolicited email promising guaranteed returns of 20% per month on a private lending investment opportunity. The email requests an upfront fee for loan processing, but after paying the fee, the investor never hears from the scammer again, and the promised loan never materializes.

2. Warning Signs of Scams and Fraud

- **Unsolicited Offers**: Be wary of unsolicited emails, phone calls, or social media messages promoting lucrative investment opportunities. Legitimate lenders typically do not solicit business through unsolicited communications and prioritize building relationships based on trust and credibility.

- **Pressure to Act Quickly**: Scammers often use high-pressure tactics to coerce investors into making hasty decisions without adequate due diligence. Beware of offers that require immediate action or claim to be time-sensitive, as this could be a tactic to prevent investors from conducting proper research.

- **Guaranteed Returns**: Exercise caution when presented with investment opportunities that promise guaranteed returns or unusually high rates of return with minimal risk. All investments carry some degree of risk, and offers that sound too good to be true are likely fraudulent or unsustainable.

- **Lack of Transparency**: Avoid deals that lack transparency or documentation, such as vague investment proposals, incomplete contracts, or refusal to provide detailed information about the investment opportunity. Legitimate lenders prioritize transparency and provide clear documentation to investors.

Note:

A borrower receives an unsolicited phone call from a lender offering a large loan at a low interest rate with no credit check required. The lender pressures the borrower to provide personal and financial information immediately to secure the loan, but the borrower becomes suspicious and hangs up.

3. Strategies to Avoid Scams and Fraud

- **Conduct Due Diligence**: Thoroughly research lenders, investment opportunities, and platforms before committing capital. Verify the legitimacy of lenders by checking their credentials, licenses, and regulatory status. Review online reviews, testimonials, and ratings to assess the reputation and track record of potential partners.

- **Seek Professional Advice**: Consult with financial advisors, legal experts, or industry professionals before making investment decisions. Experienced professionals can provide valuable insights, identify potential red flags, and help investors navigate complex lending arrangements.

- **Read and Understand Contracts**: Carefully review all documentation, including loan agreements, partnership agreements, and prospectuses, before signing. Pay attention to terms and conditions, fees, repayment schedules, and recourse mechanisms to ensure alignment with your investment objectives and risk tolerance.

- **Stay Informed**: Stay informed about common scams and fraud schemes in the private lending industry by following news updates, regulatory alerts, and industry publications. Educate yourself about warning signs and best practices for identifying and avoiding fraudulent activities.

Note:

An investor considering a private lending opportunity conducts extensive due diligence on the lending platform, including reviewing regulatory filings, checking licenses, and researching the management team. After consulting with a financial advisor and carefully reviewing the investment documentation, the investor proceeds with confidence.

4. Reporting Suspected Fraud

- **Contact Authorities**: If you encounter suspected scams or fraudulent activities, report them to relevant authorities, such as the Federal Trade Commission (FTC), Securities and Exchange Commission (SEC), or Consumer Financial Protection Bureau (CFPB). Reporting fraud helps protect other investors and may lead to enforcement actions against perpetrators.

- **File Complaints**: File complaints with appropriate regulatory agencies, law enforcement authorities, or consumer protection organizations to document your concerns and seek assistance in resolving disputes or recovering losses. Provide detailed information and documentation to support your complaint.

- **Educate Others**: Share your experiences and knowledge about scams and fraud with friends, family, and community members to raise awareness and prevent others from falling victim to similar schemes. Educating others about common red flags and best practices can help empower individuals to make informed investment decisions.

Note:

An investor who suspects fraudulent activity involving a private lending opportunity reports their concerns to the FTC and submits a complaint detailing the suspicious behavior. By taking action and alerting authorities to potential scams, the investor contributes to efforts to combat fraud and protect the integrity of the lending industry.

5. Case Study: Avoiding a Phantom Loan Scam

Scenario: A borrower receives an unsolicited email offering a large loan with favorable terms and no credit check required. The borrower suspects it may be a scam and takes steps to verify the legitimacy of the offer.

Implementation:

1. **Due Diligence**: The borrower researches the lender's website, credentials, and regulatory status to verify their legitimacy.

Check out these two free guides that I prepared for investors that may help you, as a private lender, be prepared to answer these questions:

- Uncover the 27 Red Flag Statements to Spot Fake Private And Hard Money Lenders Instantly!

  https://y2lending.com/guides

- Discover the 21 Essential Questions to Identify Legitimate Private and Hard Money Lenders and Avoid Scams!

  https://y2lending.com/guides

10.2 Borrower Bankruptcy

Borrower bankruptcy is a significant risk in private lending that can result in substantial losses for lenders.

When borrowers file for bankruptcy, they seek legal protection from creditors and may be relieved of their obligation to repay outstanding debts.

Let's explore the impact of borrower bankruptcy on private lenders, warning signs to watch out for, and strategies to mitigate risks and protect investments.

1. Understanding Borrower Bankruptcy

- **Legal Process**: Bankruptcy is a legal process that allows individuals or businesses to seek relief from overwhelming debts by restructuring or eliminating their obligations under the supervision of a bankruptcy court. Common types of bankruptcy filings include Chapter 7, Chapter 11, and Chapter 13, each with its own implications for lenders.

- **Automatic Stay**: When a borrower files for bankruptcy, an automatic stay goes into effect, halting all collection activities and legal proceedings against the borrower. This prevents lenders from pursuing repayment of debts outside the bankruptcy process and provides the borrower with temporary relief from creditor actions.

- **Discharge of Debts**: In certain bankruptcy cases, borrowers may be granted a discharge of their debts, relieving them of the legal obligation to repay qualifying debts. While secured debts may still be subject to repayment or asset forfeiture, unsecured debts may be discharged entirely, resulting in losses for lenders.

Note:

A borrower who experiences financial hardship due to job loss files for Chapter 7 bankruptcy, seeking to eliminate outstanding debts, including a personal loan from a private lender. The bankruptcy court grants a discharge of the borrower's unsecured debts, including the loan from the private lender, leaving the lender with no recourse for repayment.

2. Warning Signs of Borrower Bankruptcy

- **Financial Distress**: Watch for signs of financial distress in borrowers, such as missed payments, late fees, or requests for loan modifications. These may indicate underlying financial difficulties that could lead to bankruptcy filings.

- **Legal Notices**: Pay attention to legal notices or communications indicating potential bankruptcy filings by borrowers, such as notices of foreclosure, wage garnishment, or creditor actions. These may signal impending bankruptcy proceedings and the need for lenders to take protective measures.

- **Credit Report Changes**: Monitor changes in borrowers' credit reports, including significant increases in debt levels, credit inquiries, or accounts in collections. These changes may indicate financial instability and increased risk of bankruptcy filings.

Note:

A lender notices that a borrower has missed multiple loan payments and received notices of delinquency from other creditors. After reviewing the borrower's credit report, the lender observes a recent increase in debt levels and multiple accounts in collections, raising concerns about the borrower's financial stability and potential bankruptcy risk.

3. Strategies to Mitigate Risks of Borrower Bankruptcy

- **Conduct Due Diligence**: Thoroughly assess borrowers' creditworthiness and financial stability before extending loans, including verifying income, employment history, credit scores, and debt-to-income ratios. Select borrowers with strong financial profiles and a demonstrated ability to repay debts.

- **Secure Collateral**: Secure loans with collateral, such as real estate, vehicles, or other valuable assets, to provide recourse in the event of borrower default or bankruptcy. Collateralized loans have priority claims in bankruptcy proceedings and may increase the likelihood of recovering losses.

- **Diversify Loan Portfolio**: Diversify loan investments across multiple borrowers, industries, and asset classes to spread risk and minimize the impact of individual borrower bankruptcies. Avoid overconcentration in high-risk sectors or borrowers with limited financial stability.

- **Maintain Reserves**: Set aside reserves or provisions to account for potential losses from borrower bankruptcies. Building a cushion of funds can help offset losses and maintain liquidity during periods of economic uncertainty or borrower defaults.

Note:

A private lender adopts a conservative lending approach, carefully screening borrowers and securing loans with collateral to mitigate risks of borrower bankruptcy. By diversifying investments across multiple loans and maintaining adequate reserves, the lender prepares for potential losses and protects their investment portfolio.

4. Responding to Borrower Bankruptcy

- **Legal Representation**: Seek legal advice and representation from qualified professionals familiar with bankruptcy law and creditor rights. Consult with attorneys specializing in bankruptcy proceedings to understand your rights, obligations, and potential courses of action as a creditor.

- **Participate in Bankruptcy Proceedings**: Actively participate in bankruptcy proceedings by filing proofs of claim, attending hearings, and engaging with the bankruptcy trustee or debtor-in-possession. Stay informed about developments in the case and advocate for your interests as a creditor.

- **Explore Settlement Options**: Consider negotiating settlements or repayment agreements with borrowers or bankruptcy trustees to recover a portion of outstanding debts. Explore alternatives to litigation, such as debt restructuring, asset sales, or payment plans, to reach mutually beneficial resolutions.

Note:

A private lender engages legal counsel to represent their interests in a borrower's Chapter 11 bankruptcy proceedings. The lender files a proof of claim with the bankruptcy court, participates in creditor meetings, and explores settlement options with the debtor's estate to recover as much of the outstanding debt as possible.

5. Case Study: Mitigating Losses from Borrower Bankruptcy

Scenario: A private lender extends a loan to a borrower to finance a real estate project. The borrower experiences financial difficulties and files for Chapter 7 bankruptcy, leaving the lender at risk of significant losses.

Implementation:

1. **Due Diligence**: The lender conducts thorough due diligence on the borrower's financial status, credit history, and project feasibility before extending the loan.

2. **Collateral Protection**: The loan is secured with a first lien on the property

10.3 Overcommitting Funds

Overcommitting funds is a common pitfall in private lending where lenders allocate more capital than prudent to loans or investment opportunities. It's often leading to increased risk and potential losses.

Let's explore the risks associated with overcommitting funds, warning signs to watch out for, and strategies to avoid overcommitment and maintain a balanced lending portfolio.

1. Understanding Overcommitting Funds

- **Capital Allocation**: Overcommitting funds occurs when lenders allocate a disproportionate amount of their capital to loans or investments, exceeding their risk tolerance or capacity to absorb potential losses. This may result from a desire to maximize returns, lack of diversification, or underestimation of risk factors.

- **Increased Exposure**: Overcommitting funds increases lenders' exposure to individual loans, borrowers, or sectors, amplifying the impact of adverse events such as borrower defaults, economic downturns, or market volatility. Concentrated exposure heightens risk and reduces portfolio resilience.

- **Liquidity Constraints**: Overcommitment may restrict lenders' liquidity and ability to respond to unforeseen events or opportunities. Tying up a significant portion of capital in illiquid loans or investments limits flexibility and may hinder portfolio management and risk mitigation efforts.

Note:

A private lender allocates a substantial portion of their available capital to a single high-risk loan opportunity, hoping to earn attractive returns. However, when the borrower defaults on the loan, the lender faces significant losses due to overcommitting funds to the risky investment.

2. Warning Signs of Overcommitting Funds

- **High Concentration**: Watch for high concentration levels in loan investments, borrower profiles, or asset classes within the lending portfolio. Overly concentrated positions increase vulnerability to adverse events and limit diversification benefits.

- **Limited Risk Assessment**: Pay attention to limited risk assessment or due diligence conducted on loans or investment opportunities. Inadequate analysis of borrower creditworthiness, collateral quality, or market conditions may indicate a lack of consideration for potential risks.

- **Aggressive Investment Strategies**: Be cautious of aggressive investment strategies that prioritize maximizing returns over prudent risk management. Strategies such as chasing high-yield opportunities, leveraging capital, or ignoring risk factors may increase the likelihood of overcommitment.

- **Lack of Exit Strategy**: Lack of a clear exit strategy or contingency plan for loans or investments may signal overcommitment. Without predefined exit options, lenders may find it challenging to unwind positions or mitigate losses in the event of adverse developments.

Note:

A private lender notices that a significant portion of their loan portfolio is concentrated in a single sector, with limited diversification across industries or asset classes. Despite warning signs of sector-specific risks, the lender continues to allocate funds to similar high-risk loans, increasing exposure and overcommitment.

3. Strategies to Avoid Overcommitting Funds

- **Risk-Based Allocation**: Implement a risk-based approach to capital allocation, considering factors such as borrower creditworthiness, loan collateral, and industry risk. Allocate capital prudently based on risk-return profiles, diversification objectives, and risk tolerance levels.

- **Portfolio Diversification**: Diversify investments across multiple loans, borrowers, industries, and asset classes to spread risk and minimize the impact of individual defaults or market fluctuations. Maintain a balanced portfolio mix to reduce concentration risk and enhance resilience.

- **Stress Testing**: Conduct stress tests and scenario analyzes to assess the potential impact of adverse events on the lending portfolio. Evaluate the sensitivity of portfolio performance to various risk factors and adjust capital allocation accordingly to mitigate overcommitment risks.

- **Liquidity Management**: Manage liquidity effectively by maintaining sufficient reserves and flexibility to respond to changing market conditions or unexpected events. Avoid tying up all available capital in illiquid investments and prioritize maintaining liquidity buffers to support ongoing operations and risk management.

Note:

A private lender adopts a disciplined approach to capital allocation, diversifying investments across multiple loans and sectors based on risk assessment and diversification principles. By regularly monitoring portfolio concentration levels and stress-testing portfolio resilience, the lender avoids overcommitment and maintains a balanced lending portfolio.

4. Responding to Overcommitment Risks

- **Portfolio Rebalancing**: Assess portfolio composition regularly and rebalance capital allocation to align with risk management objectives and market conditions. Adjust investment allocations, reduce exposure to high-risk positions, and reallocate capital to underweighted areas to mitigate overcommitment risks.

- **Risk Mitigation Measures**: Implement risk mitigation measures such as collateral enhancement, loan restructuring, or asset disposition to reduce exposure to overcommitted positions. Actively manage high-risk loans or investments to minimize potential losses and preserve portfolio value.

- **Continuous Monitoring**: Monitor portfolio performance and market developments continuously to identify emerging risks and opportunities. Stay informed about changes in borrower creditworthiness, market trends, and regulatory developments that may impact portfolio risk levels and require proactive adjustments.

Note:

A private lender identifies overcommitment risks in their loan portfolio and takes proactive measures to rebalance capital allocation and mitigate concentration risks. By reducing exposure to high-risk positions, implementing risk mitigation measures, and maintaining vigilant monitoring, the lender effectively manages overcommitment risks and maintains portfolio stability.

5. Case Study: Mitigating Overcommitment Risks

Scenario: A private lender notices that a significant portion of their loan portfolio is concentrated in a single industry, increasing exposure to sector-specific risks and potential overcommitment.

Implementation:

1. **Portfolio Analysis**: The lender conducts a comprehensive analysis of their loan portfolio, assessing concentration levels, risk exposures, and diversification gaps.

2. **Rebalancing Strategy**: Based on the portfolio analysis, the lender develops a rebalancing strategy to reduce exposure to the high-risk industry and reallocate capital to underweighted sectors.

3. **Diversification Plan**: The lender diversifies investments across multiple industries, borrowers, and asset classes to spread risk and minimize overcommitment.

4. **Ongoing Monitoring**: The lender monitors portfolio performance continuously, adjusting capital allocation and rebalancing positions as needed to maintain a balanced and resilient lending portfolio.

CHAPTER 11

THE FUTURE OF
PRIVATE LENDING

11.1 Trends and Innovations

The future of private lending is shaped by evolving market dynamics, technological advancements, and changing borrower preferences.

Let's explore emerging trends and innovations in the private lending industry, including technological disruptions, regulatory developments, and shifts in borrower behavior, shaping the landscape for lenders and investors.

1. Technological Disruptions

- **Online Platforms**: The rise of online lending platforms has transformed the private lending landscape, enabling borrowers to access financing quickly and conveniently while providing investors with opportunities to participate in loan investments through digital channels.

- **Peer-to-Peer Lending**: Peer-to-peer (P2P) lending platforms connect borrowers directly with individual investors, bypassing traditional financial intermediaries. P2P lending offers borrowers competitive rates and investors attractive returns, driving growth in the alternative lending market.

- **Blockchain and Smart Contracts**: Blockchain technology and smart contracts have the potential to streamline loan origination, underwriting, and servicing processes, reducing costs, enhancing transparency, and mitigating fraud risks in private lending transactions.

Note:

A private lending platform leverages blockchain technology to facilitate secure, transparent, and efficient loan transactions. Smart contracts automate loan agreements, enforce terms, and facilitate seamless payments, enhancing trust and reducing administrative overhead for borrowers and investors.

2. Regulatory Developments

- **Compliance Frameworks**: Regulatory frameworks governing private lending continue to evolve, with policymakers seeking to strike a balance between promoting innovation and protecting investors and borrowers. Lenders must navigate complex regulatory requirements and compliance obligations to operate legally and ethically.

- **Consumer Protection**: Regulators focus on consumer protection measures to safeguard borrower interests and ensure fair lending practices in the private lending market. Enhanced disclosure requirements, interest rate caps, and borrower eligibility criteria aim to mitigate risks and prevent predatory lending practices.

- **Market Oversight**: Regulatory authorities monitor private lending activities closely, imposing licensing, registration, and reporting requirements on lenders and platforms. Increased oversight aims to promote market integrity, transparency, and accountability while deterring fraudulent activities and misconduct.

Note:

A private lending platform adapts to regulatory changes by enhancing compliance measures, implementing robust risk management practices, and adopting industry best practices for consumer protection and market integrity. By prioritizing regulatory compliance, the platform maintains trust and credibility with stakeholders.

3. Shifts in Borrower Behavior

- **Preference for Digital Solutions**: Borrowers increasingly favor digital lending platforms that offer speed, convenience, and transparency in the loan application and approval process. Online platforms provide borrowers with access to a wide range of financing options and competitive terms, driving adoption and market growth.

- **Demand for Alternative Financing**: As traditional lending sources become more restrictive or inaccessible, borrowers turn to alternative financing options such as private lending, peer-to-peer lending, and crowdfunding to meet their funding needs. Alternative lenders fill gaps in the market and cater to underserved borrower segments.

- **Customized Loan Products**: Borrowers seek customized loan products tailored to their specific needs, preferences, and financial circumstances. Flexible terms, personalized pricing, and innovative loan structures empower borrowers to choose financing solutions that align with their goals and constraints.

Note:

A borrower applies for a loan through an online lending platform, attracted by competitive interest rates, streamlined application process, and personalized loan options. The borrower receives multiple loan offers from investors on the platform, selecting the most favorable terms that meet their financing needs.

4. Market Expansion and Globalization

- **Geographic Reach**: Private lending platforms expand their geographic reach to serve borrowers and investors in diverse markets worldwide. Globalization opens up new opportunities for cross-border lending, investment diversification, and access to untapped borrower segments.

- **Sectoral Focus**: Lenders specialize in niche sectors such as real estate, small business, consumer finance, and healthcare, catering to specific borrower segments and industry needs. Sector-focused lending platforms offer tailored financing solutions and expertise to address sector-specific challenges and opportunities.

- **International Partnerships**: Lenders form strategic partnerships and alliances with financial institutions, technology firms, and regulatory authorities to facilitate cross-border lending, regulatory compliance, and market expansion initiatives. Collaborative efforts promote innovation, knowledge sharing, and market development in the private lending ecosystem.

Note:

A private lending platform enters into a partnership with a foreign financial institution to facilitate cross-border lending between investors and borrowers in different countries. By leveraging the partner's local expertise, regulatory knowledge, and market presence, the platform expands its global footprint and enhances market access for participants.

5. Embracing ESG Principles

- **Environmental, Social, and Governance (ESG) Integration:** Private lenders increasingly incorporate ESG factors into their lending practices, evaluating the environmental, social, and governance impacts of loan investments. ESG integration aligns lending activities with sustainability goals, risk management objectives, and stakeholder expectations.

- **Impact Investing:** Investors seek opportunities to deploy capital in private lending projects that generate positive social and environmental outcomes alongside financial returns. Impact investing initiatives support initiatives such as affordable housing, renewable energy, healthcare access, and community development, driving social change and value creation.

- **Stakeholder Engagement:** Lenders engage with borrowers, investors, regulators, and other stakeholders to promote ESG awareness, transparency, and accountability in the private lending ecosystem. Collaborative efforts foster dialogue, knowledge sharing, and best practices adoption to advance sustainability goals and responsible lending principles.

Note:

A private lending firm adopts an ESG framework to assess the environmental, social, and governance impacts of its loan portfolio. The firm integrates ESG considerations into investment decision-making, risk assessment, and portfolio management processes, aligning lending activities with sustainability objectives and stakeholder expectations.

By embracing emerging trends and innovations, you, as a private lender, can adapt to evolving market dynamics, meet the needs of borrowers and investors, and drive positive outcomes in the dynamic and competitive private lending landscape.

11.2 Global Opportunities

The future of private lending holds immense potential for expansion and growth on a global scale, driven by increasing demand for alternative financing solutions, technological advancements, and evolving regulatory landscapes.

Let's explore the opportunities presented by global markets for private lenders, including market expansion strategies, cross-border lending initiatives, and partnerships to capitalize on international growth prospects.

1. Market Expansion Strategies

- **Geographic Diversification**: Private lenders seek opportunities to diversify their lending activities across multiple geographic regions to spread risk, access new borrower segments, and capitalize on market growth prospects. Expanding into international markets offers diversification benefits and enhances resilience against regional economic fluctuations.

- **Emerging Markets**: Emerging economies present attractive opportunities for private lending, fueled by rapid urbanization, population growth, and rising demand for infrastructure development, housing, and consumer finance. Emerging markets offer higher growth potential, but also pose unique risks and challenges that require careful consideration and risk management.

Note:

A private lending platform based in the United States expands its operations into Latin America, targeting emerging markets such as Brazil, Mexico, and Colombia. By leveraging its technology, expertise, and network, the platform connects investors with borrowers in Latin America, facilitating cross-border lending and capitalizing on growth opportunities in the region.

2. Cross-Border Lending Initiatives

- **Global Connectivity**: Technological advancements and digital platforms enable cross-border lending initiatives, connecting investors and borrowers across different countries and continents. Cross-border lending facilitates capital flow, enhances investment diversification, and broadens access to financing for borrowers worldwide.

- **Regulatory Considerations**: Cross-border lending involves navigating complex regulatory frameworks, compliance requirements, and legal considerations in multiple jurisdictions. Lenders must understand regulatory differences, obtain necessary licenses or approvals, and comply with local laws to operate legally and ethically in international markets.

Note:

A private lending firm based in Europe partners with a peer-to-peer lending platform in Asia to facilitate cross-border lending between European investors and Asian borrowers. The partnership leverages technology, regulatory expertise, and market knowledge to enable seamless loan transactions and expand access to financing across regions.

3. Strategic Partnerships

- **International Collaborations**: Strategic partnerships and alliances with local financial institutions, technology firms, and regulatory authorities enhance lenders' capabilities to enter and operate in international markets. Collaborative efforts leverage complementary strengths, resources, and expertise to overcome market entry barriers and accelerate growth.

- **Market Access**: Partnerships provide lenders with access to local markets, distribution channels, and customer networks, enabling them to reach a broader audience of borrowers and investors. Joint ventures, licensing agreements, and distribution partnerships facilitate market penetration and expansion into new territories.

Note:

A private lending platform based in Asia forms a strategic partnership with a European bank to launch a cross-border lending initiative targeting small and medium-sized enterprises (SMEs). The partnership combines the platform's technology and market reach with the bank's regulatory compliance and local market presence to offer financing solutions to SMEs in Europe and Asia.

4. Sectoral Focus and Specialization

- **Industry Expertise**: Private lenders specialize in niche sectors such as real estate, renewable energy, healthcare, and fintech, leveraging industry expertise to identify unique investment opportunities and address specific borrower needs. Sector-focused lending strategies enable lenders to differentiate their offerings, mitigate risks, and capitalize on sectoral growth trends.

- **Global Megatrends**: Global megatrends such as urbanization, sustainability, digitalization, and demographic shifts drive demand for specialized financing solutions in key sectors worldwide. Lenders align their lending activities with these megatrends, investing in projects and initiatives that address critical challenges and opportunities shaping the global economy.

Note:

A private lending firm specializing in renewable energy financing expands its operations globally to capitalize on the growing demand for clean energy projects. The firm partners with developers, governments, and international organizations to fund solar, wind, and hydroelectric projects in emerging markets, contributing to the transition towards sustainable energy systems.

5. Risk Management and Due Diligence

- **International Risks**: Global expansion introduces new risks and challenges related to political instability, currency fluctuations, legal uncertainties, and cultural differences. Lenders must conduct thorough risk assessments, due diligence, and scenario analyses to identify and mitigate risks associated with international operations.

- **Local Partnerships**: Collaborating with local partners, advisors, and consultants familiar with the nuances of international markets enhances lenders' understanding of local conditions, regulatory environments, and business practices. Local expertise complements lenders' capabilities and strengthens risk management frameworks for international lending activities.

Note:

A private lending platform entering the African market partners with local legal firms, financial advisors, and regulatory experts to navigate regulatory complexities, assess country-specific risks, and ensure compliance with local laws and regulations. The partnership facilitates market entry and mitigates risks associated with operating in unfamiliar jurisdictions.

6. Case Study: Expanding into Emerging Markets

Scenario: A private lending platform based in North America seeks to expand its operations into emerging markets in Southeast Asia to capitalize on growing demand for alternative financing solutions.

Implementation:

1. **Market Research**: The platform conducts extensive market research to assess market dynamics, regulatory frameworks, and competitive landscapes in target countries such as Indonesia, Thailand, and Vietnam.

2. **Partnership Development**: The platform establishes partnerships with local financial institutions, technology providers, and regulatory authorities to navigate regulatory

requirements, obtain necessary licenses, and access local market insights.

3. **Technology Integration**: The platform leverages its technology infrastructure to adapt its lending platform to local languages, currencies, and regulatory requirements, ensuring seamless user experience and compliance with local regulations.

4. **Risk Management**: The platform implements robust risk management practices, including credit risk assessment, collateral evaluation, and regulatory compliance, to mitigate risks associated with operating in emerging markets.

5. **Market Entry**: The platform launches its lending services in Southeast Asia, targeting underserved borrower segments such as SMEs, microenterprises

11.3 Sustainable and Ethical Lending

The future of private lending is increasingly shaped by sustainability principles and ethical considerations, as lenders recognize the importance of aligning financial activities with environmental, social, and governance (ESG) goals.

Let's explore the growing emphasis on sustainable and ethical lending practices, including impact investing initiatives, ESG integration strategies, and responsible lending principles driving positive social and environmental outcomes.

1. Impact Investing Initiatives

- **Social Impact**: Private lenders play a crucial role in addressing social challenges and driving positive change through impact investing initiatives. Impact investing focuses on financing projects and businesses that generate measurable social and environmental benefits alongside financial returns, supporting initiatives such as affordable housing, healthcare access, and education.

- **Environmental Sustainability**: Lenders prioritize environmental sustainability by funding projects and initiatives that promote renewable energy, climate resilience, and conservation efforts. Sustainable lending practices aim to mitigate climate change, reduce carbon emissions, and protect natural resources, contributing to a more sustainable and resilient future.

Note:

A private lending firm partners with a nonprofit organization to fund affordable housing projects in underserved communities. The lending firm provides financing for the development of energy-efficient, affordable housing units, addressing housing affordability challenges while promoting environmental sustainability through green building practices.

2. ESG Integration Strategies

- **Risk Management**: Private lenders integrate ESG factors into their risk management frameworks to assess the environmental, social, and governance risks associated with loan investments. ESG integration enhances risk identification, measurement, and mitigation capabilities, enabling lenders to make informed decisions and protect their investments.

- **Stakeholder Engagement**: Lenders engage with borrowers, investors, regulators, and other stakeholders to promote ESG awareness, transparency, and accountability in the lending process. Stakeholder engagement fosters dialogue, collaboration, and knowledge sharing, driving continuous improvement in ESG practices and performance.

Note:

A private lending platform incorporates ESG criteria into its loan underwriting process, evaluating borrowers based on their environmental practices, social impact, and governance structures. The platform engages with borrowers to encourage ESG best practices, provide resources for sustainability initiatives, and track ESG performance over time.

3. Responsible Lending Principles

- **Fair and Transparent Practices**: Lenders adhere to fair and transparent lending practices, ensuring that borrowers receive clear and accurate information about loan terms, fees, and repayment obligations. Responsible lending principles prioritize consumer protection, financial inclusion, and ethical conduct throughout the lending lifecycle.

- **Avoidance of Predatory Practices**: Lenders refrain from engaging in predatory lending practices that exploit vulnerable borrowers or impose unfair terms and conditions. Responsible lenders assess borrowers' ability to repay loans, offer affordable and sustainable financing options, and provide support to borrowers facing financial difficulties.

Note:

A private lending institution adopts a responsible lending policy that emphasizes fair treatment of borrowers, ethical conduct, and compliance with regulatory requirements. The institution implements safeguards to prevent predatory practices, such as usury limits, disclosure requirements, and borrower education initiatives, to promote responsible lending standards.

4. Green Financing and Climate Resilience

- **Green Loans**: Private lenders offer green financing solutions to fund projects and initiatives that promote environmental sustainability and combat climate change. Green loans support investments in renewable energy, energy efficiency, sustainable transportation, and green infrastructure, facilitating the transition to a low-carbon economy.

- **Climate Resilience**: Lenders prioritize climate resilience by funding projects and initiatives that enhance resilience to climate-related risks and disasters. Climate-resilient investments include infrastructure upgrades, disaster preparedness measures, and community resilience initiatives, protecting assets and communities from the impacts of climate change.

Note:

A private lending consortium provides financing for a solar energy project in a developing country, supporting the deployment of clean, renewable energy sources and reducing reliance on fossil fuels. The project contributes to environmental sustainability by reducing carbon emissions and promoting energy access and resilience in the local community.

5. Measuring Impact and Reporting

- **Impact Measurement**: Private lenders develop metrics and methodologies to measure the social, environmental, and economic impact of their lending activities. Impact measurement frameworks assess outcomes, track progress towards sustainability goals, and demonstrate the positive contributions of lending initiatives to stakeholders.

- **Transparency and Reporting**: Lenders prioritize transparency and reporting on ESG performance, providing stakeholders with access to relevant data, metrics, and impact reports. Transparent reporting enhances accountability, builds trust with stakeholders, and enables informed decision-making on sustainability and ethical lending practices.

Note:

A private lending firm publishes an annual impact report highlighting the social, environmental, and economic impact of its lending portfolio. The impact report includes quantitative and qualitative data on key performance indicators, case studies, and testimonials from borrowers and communities, demonstrating the firm's commitment to sustainability and ethical lending.

By integrating sustainability principles into lending activities, you, as a private lender, can create positive social and environmental impact, mitigate risks, and contribute to a more inclusive, resilient, and sustainable financial system.

CHAPTER 12

CONCLUSION

12.1 Summary of Key Points

This summary serves as a quick reference, reinforcing the main concepts and actionable steps that aspiring private lenders can take to succeed in the industry.

Here, we highlight the key points from each chapter to provide a comprehensive overview.

1. Introduction to Private Lending

- **Definition and Overview**: Private lending involves individuals or entities providing loans to borrowers without going through traditional financial institutions.

- **Benefits**: Offers higher returns, diversification, and flexibility.

- **Risks**: Includes default risk, market volatility, and liquidity issues.

- **Historical Context**: Private lending has roots in ancient civilizations and has evolved significantly over time.

2. The Mechanics of Private Lending

- **Loan Basics**: Understand the fundamental components of a loan, including principal, interest, term, and repayment schedule.

- **Types of Private Loans**: Differentiates between secured, unsecured, short-term, and long-term loans.

- **Risk Assessment**: Identifies methods to evaluate and mitigate risks, emphasizing the importance of thorough due diligence.

- **Setting Interest Rates**: Factors influencing interest rates include borrower creditworthiness, loan term, and market conditions

3. Active vs. Passive Private Lending

- **Active Lending**: Involves direct interaction with borrowers, active management of loans, and requires more time and effort.

- **Passive Lending**: Includes investments in funds, P2P platforms, or becoming a silent partner, offering a more hands-off approach.

4. Legal and Regulatory Considerations

- **Legal Requirements**: Compliance with federal and state regulations, licensing, and understanding usury laws.

- **Creating Lending Agreements**: Importance of clear, legally binding contracts detailing terms, conditions, and recourse in case of default.

- **Finding Borrowers**: Strategies for identifying and vetting potential borrowers, leveraging networks, and marketing.

5. Evaluating Borrowers and Loans

- **Credit Scores and Reports**: Using credit information to assess borrower reliability and risk.

- **Assessing Risk**: Techniques for evaluating borrower risk, including financial statements, collateral, and industry analysis.

- **Setting Interest Rates**: Balancing competitive rates with risk management to ensure profitability and borrower affordability.

6. Learning from History

- **Historical Case Study: J.P. Morgan**: Insights from J.P. Morgan's approach to private lending and risk management.

- **Modern Success Stories**: Examples of contemporary private lenders who have successfully navigated the industry.
- **Lessons Learned**: Key takeaways from historical and modern examples to apply to current lending practices.

7. Managing Your Loans

- **Monitoring Payments**: Techniques for tracking loan repayments, using technology to automate and streamline processes.

- **Dealing with Late Payments**: Strategies for handling delinquencies, including communication, restructuring, and legal action.

- **Legal Actions**: Steps to take when pursuing legal recourse for defaulted loans, including foreclosure, repossession, and litigation.

8. Growing Your Private Lending Business

- **Reinvesting Profits**: Strategies for reinvesting earnings to grow your lending portfolio and increase returns.

- **Networking**: Building relationships with other lenders, industry professionals, and potential borrowers to expand opportunities.

- **Diversifying Your Portfolio**: Importance of diversification across different loan types, industries, and geographic regions to mitigate risk.

9. Passive Lending Options

- **Peer-to-Peer Lending Platforms**: Understanding the workings, benefits, and risks of P2P lending.

- **Investing in Private Lending Funds**: Advantages of pooled investment funds for diversification and professional management.

- **Becoming a Silent Partner**: Providing capital to businesses without involvement in day-to-day operations, focusing on profit sharing.

10. Common Pitfalls and How to Avoid Them

- **Scams and Fraud**: Identifying and protecting against common fraudulent schemes and ensuring due diligence.

- **Borrower Bankruptcy**: Understanding the implications of borrower bankruptcy and strategies for minimizing impact.

- **Overcommitting Funds**: Avoiding the risk of over-leverage by maintaining liquidity and prudent capital allocation.

11. The Future of Private Lending

- **Trends and Innovations**: Embracing technological advancements, regulatory changes, and evolving market dynamics.

- **Global Opportunities**: Exploring international markets for diversification and growth potential.

- **Sustainable and Ethical Lending**: Integrating ESG principles into lending practices to drive positive social and environmental impact.

12. Conclusion

- **Reflection**: Recap of the journey through private lending, emphasizing the blend of opportunities and responsibilities.

- **Actionable Steps**: Encouragement to apply the knowledge gained, continue learning, and adapt to changes in the industry.

- **Future Outlook**: A positive yet realistic perspective on the potential growth and evolution of private lending.

This summary of key points underscores the critical areas covered in the book, offering readers a clear roadmap to becoming successful private lenders. By understanding and applying these insights, aspiring lenders can navigate the complexities of the industry, mitigate risks, and achieve their financial goals.

12.2 Summary of Links

Explore opportunities to become a passive private money lender:

- Y2 Capital Group Debt Fund

  http://y2lending.com/invest

Check out these two free guides that I prepared for investors that may help you, as a private lender, be prepared to answer their questions:

- Uncover the 27 Red Flag Statements to Spot Fake Private And Hard Money Lenders Instantly!

https://y2lending.com/guides

- Discover the 21 Essential Questions to Identify Legitimate Private and Hard Money Lenders and Avoid Scams!

https://y2lending.com/guides

12.3 Next Steps

As you conclude your journey through "The Definitive Guide to Making Money as a Private Lender," it's time to turn knowledge into action.

Here are some practical steps to help you get started and succeed as a private lender.

By following these actionable steps, you can establish a solid foundation, build your lending business, and achieve financial success.

1. Assess Your Financial Situation

- **Evaluate Your Finances**: Start by taking a close look at your current financial situation. Determine how much capital you have available for lending and how much you can comfortably allocate without compromising your financial stability.

- **Set Financial Goals**: Define clear financial goals for your private lending activities. Whether you aim to generate passive income, diversify your investment portfolio, or support community projects, having specific goals will guide your lending decisions.

Note:

You might set a goal to allocate 20% of your investment portfolio to private lending, aiming to achieve an annual return of 8-10%.

2. Educate Yourself Continuously

- **Stay Informed**: The private lending industry is dynamic and continuously evolving. Stay informed about market trends, regulatory changes, and new lending practices by reading industry publications, attending seminars, and joining professional associations.

- **Expand Your Knowledge**: Deepen your understanding of financial analysis, risk management, and loan structuring through online courses, workshops, and certification programs. Continuous learning will enhance your skills and confidence as a private lender.

Note:

Enroll in a course on financial risk assessment or attend a conference focused on alternative lending to stay updated on the latest industry developments.

3. Develop a Business Plan

- **Create a Strategy**: Outline your private lending strategy, including target markets, loan types, interest rates, and risk management practices. A well-defined business plan will serve as a roadmap for your lending activities and help you stay focused on your goals.

- **Set Policies and Procedures**: Establish clear policies and procedures for loan origination, underwriting, servicing, and collections. Standardized processes will ensure consistency, efficiency, and compliance with regulatory requirements.

Note:

Draft a business plan that includes a mission statement, target borrower profile, loan terms, risk assessment criteria, and marketing strategies.

4. Build Your Network

- **Connect with Industry Professionals**: Networking is crucial in the private lending industry. Build relationships with other lenders, brokers, financial advisors, and legal experts who can provide valuable insights, referrals, and support.

- **Join Associations**: Become a member of professional associations and organizations related to private lending and real estate finance. These associations offer networking opportunities, resources, and advocacy to help you succeed.

Note:

Join the National Private Lenders Association (NPLA) or a local real estate investment group to connect with like-minded professionals and stay informed about industry trends.

5. Implement Technology Solutions

- **Adopt Digital Tools**: Leverage technology to streamline your lending operations. Use online platforms for loan origination, underwriting software for credit analysis, and automated systems for loan servicing and payment tracking.

- **Enhance Security**: Implement robust cybersecurity measures to protect sensitive borrower information and financial data. Ensure compliance with data protection regulations to maintain trust and credibility.

Note:

Utilize a loan management software that offers features like borrower tracking, payment reminders, and financial reporting to enhance efficiency and accuracy.

6. Start Small and Scale Up

- **Pilot Program**: Begin with a small pilot program to test your lending strategies, refine your processes, and gain practical experience. Starting small allows you to learn and make adjustments without taking on significant risk.

- **Gradual Expansion**: As you build confidence and achieve positive results, gradually expand your lending portfolio. Diversify your loans across different borrower types, loan terms, and geographic regions to mitigate risk and maximize returns.

Note:

Launch a pilot program by funding a few small loans to local businesses or real estate investors. Monitor performance, gather feedback, and use insights to improve your approach before scaling up.

7. Monitor and Adapt

- **Track Performance**: Regularly monitor the performance of your loans, including repayment rates, default rates, and return on investment. Use data analytics to identify trends, assess risk, and make informed decisions.

- **Stay Flexible:** The lending landscape can change rapidly due to economic shifts, regulatory changes, and market dynamics. Stay flexible and be prepared to adapt your strategies and business plan to navigate new challenges and seize opportunities.

Note:

Create a dashboard to track key performance indicators (KPIs) such as loan default rates, average interest rates, and portfolio diversification. Use this data to make informed adjustments to your lending strategy.

8. Seek Professional Advice

- **Consult Experts:** Work with financial advisors, legal professionals, and tax consultants to ensure compliance with regulations, optimize your tax strategy, and protect your investments. Professional advice can help you navigate complex legal and financial issues.

- **Mentorship and Coaching:** Consider finding a mentor or coach with experience in private lending. Mentorship provides valuable guidance, support, and insights that can accelerate your learning curve and enhance your success.

Note:

Schedule regular consultations with a financial advisor to review your lending portfolio, discuss risk management strategies, and explore new investment opportunities.

Conclusion

Remember, the key to thriving as a private lender lies in balancing risk and reward, maintaining ethical standards, and staying adaptable to the ever-changing financial landscape.

www.ingramcontent.com/pod-product-compliance
Lightning Source LLC
Chambersburg PA
CBHW071919210526
45479CB00002B/480